THE HEART OF THE APOSTLE

A Commentary on
Romans 9 - 11

Richard E. Freeman,
D. Min.

The Heart of The Apostle
A Commentary on Romans 9-11

Printed in the United States of America
Published by InstantPublisher.com
ISBN# 1-59872-809-5

Contents

Dedication

To my wife Julia who has been my partner in everything:

Thank you for your incredible love, encouragement, and support throughout this process.

You were always there to help me see the light at the end of the tunnel and to encourage me to continue when I wondered if I would ever finish the task.

You truly are the essence of a Proverbs 31 woman.

I am blessed to be your husband. I love you.

Introduction

What is so important about Romans 9-11? Why a commentary on only three chapters of the book of Romans? Having been involved in Jewish ministry for more than twenty years, I have come to the conclusion that these three chapters in Romans may be the most important chapters in all of Scripture for understanding the heart of the apostle to the Gentiles, Paul, as it pertained to Israel, his "brethren according to the flesh."

As the three chapters unfold, Paul reveals his broken heart over the lostness of his people. That broken heart is so significant in light of those who are teaching a double covenant, that Israel, Jewish people, will go to heaven because of their unique covenant with God through Abraham, and therefore don't need Jesus, their Messiah. In Jewish ministry, it is not uncommon to have to show Christians that Jewish people, like everyone else, are lost apart from Jesus. It is part of who we are, as we share the the burden of the broken heart of Paul over the lostness of his people with others.

As Chapter 10 begins, Paul's heart was prayerful, as we see his most heartfelt prayer for Israel was for their salvation. That prayer was an indicator that although Paul was broken hearted over Israel's lostness, he was also hopeful because God was not finished with his people.

Paul knew that Jewish people were still getting saved, and as chapter 11 began Paul used himself as a means of proving that point. He believed that through the faithful witness of his new Gentile converts, as he shares in Romans 11:11, the remnant, that small number who would respond to the gospel, would ultimately get saved.

Finally, Paul connects salvation of the Jewish people to the last days and shares his confidence that in the end, when Jesus returns to earth, those alive at the time of the event would respond to Him and accept Him as their Messiah, Savior and Lord. As the three chapters conclude we see Paul overwhelmed with the awesomeness of God as he worships the Lord.

The heart of the apostle is first seen in Chapter 9 as being broken over the lostness of his Jewish brethren. In Chapter 10 we see his heart being prayerful, as the most fervent prayer of his heart was for his Jewish brethren's salvation. In Chapter 11, Paul's heart is seen as being hopeful, as he shares what he hopes will be a "Gentile Great Commission," to provoke Israel to jealousy. We see his heart confidently trusting in the perfect plan of God, which will result in those Jewish people alive at the time of Jesus' return to earth accepting Him as the Messiah. And finally, Paul's heart rejoices in worship over the God who is able to bring all this to pass, the only one worthy of all glory. My prayer for you, as you read this book, is that you would have the heart of the apostle.

CHAPTER 1

A Broken Heart For Israel

The book of Romans is considered by many Bible scholars to be Paul's *magnum opus*, his greatest work. Some of the greatest theological teaching in the Bible is found in the first eight chapters of Romans. The end of Romans 8, from verses 31 and following, can be seen as a celebration, a celebration of God's love and faithfulness which certainly is an appropriate conclusion to Paul's teaching in Romans up to that point. Then, as the chapter concludes, one can imagine Paul stopping, taking a deep breath, and making the key statement that reflects on everything that he has taught in the letter to the Romans so far. He says, beginning in Romans 8:38-39:

> "For I am persuaded that neither death nor life, nor angels nor principalities nor powers, nor things present, nor things to come, nor height nor depth, nor any other created thing, shall be able to separate us from the love of God which is in Christ Jesus our Lord."

It would be logical to expect Paul to give practical application to his teaching in Romans 1-8 at this point; but that doesn't happen until Romans 12.

"Nothing can separate us from the love of God which is in Christ Jesus our Lord." This is a key phrase that should be an encouragement to every believer. But if these predominantly Gentile believers are going to be encouraged by this summary statement of God's faithful love and ability to save and keep us saved, a question must be answered before Paul can continue in his teaching. That question can be stated in three succinct words --- What about Israel?

To many of those who hold to a belief that is commonly called "Replacement Theology," believing that the church is the new Israel and all of the promises to Israel are now given to the church, Romans 9 through 11 is seen as being merely a parenthetical detour by Paul that interrupts the flow of the book. Romans 9 through 11 is not parenthetical, it is pivotal. It is

Paul's response to a question that must be asked by those Gentile believers who have been blessed to have "received the Spirit of adoption." How are we supposed to trust in the faithfulness of God to keep us saved if He is unable to keep Israel from falling?

To see Romans 9 through 11 as nothing more than a parenthetical ramble by Paul, is to do violence to the Scripture. Those who would say it is not worthy of spending much time in study, because clearly the church has inherited the blessings originally intended for the descendants of Abraham anyway, have not understood Paul's heart.

Romans 9 through 11 is not merely Paul answering that critical question, What about Israel? In this text, Paul, the Apostle to the Gentiles, shares the deepest burden of his heart, with his predominantly Gentile readers, regarding his Jewish brethren. In these three chapters Paul lays out his burden to see his Jewish brethren saved, as well as the role he sees for the Gentile church in helping to get that accomplished. Paul also discusses the connection between Jewish people getting saved and the last days.

These are important truths that must be communicated to the church accurately, and this commentary is intended to be a tool to help accomplish that objective. For those in Jewish missions, this is especially important if we are to accomplish our task of helping the body of Messiah, the church of Jesus Christ, to properly understand its role in Jewish evangelism.

I have divided the three chapters into eleven preaching units for this commentary, which will be helpful both in terms of understanding the Biblical text as well as in communicating the various themes that Paul is presenting. As Paul begins the job of answering the question, What about Israel? his first task is to communicate to his readers, in Romans 9:1-5, his broken heart over the lostness of his Jewish brethren. He writes in Romans 9:1-2:

> "I tell the truth in Christ, I am not lying, my conscience also bearing me witness in the Holy Spirit, that I have great sorrow and continual grief in my heart."

Why would Paul say, "I tell the truth in Christ, I am not lying, my conscience also bearing me witness in the Holy Spirit?" As this letter continues Paul is going to be getting into some very controversial subjects regarding his Jewish brethren. He is going to be talking about Israel's unbelief and their national rejection of their Messiah, and he wants to make sure he is not misunderstood. The last thing he wants is for anyone to misunderstand what he is writing and somehow assert that Paul is writing about the consequences of Israel's unbelief because he hates them. Perhaps someone might make the charge and say, "Paul is really enjoying this," considering how he's been treated by the Jewish people.

When you study Paul's missionary journeys in the book of Acts, there certainly are enough incidents of personal attacks by his Jewish brethren to possibly warrant that kind of conclusion. Paul himself, in 2 Corinthians 11:24-25 writes:

> "From the Jews five times I received forty stripes minus one. Three times I was beaten with rods; once I was stoned."

The Jewish religious leaders even went so far as to plot an assassination attempt against Paul which was thwarted by his nephew (Acts 23:16). As Paul begins this section he wants to be crystal clear of his love for Israel and for his broken heart over their lost state. This broken heart for the lostness of the Jewish people will ultimately be what Paul hopes will get transferred to his new Gentile converts.

Paul calls on both Christ and the Holy Spirit as his witnesses of the truthfulness of the assertion he is about to make. In the positive phrase, "I tell the truth in Christ," Paul is calling on the Messiah Himself as the ultimate guarantor of the truthfulness of his statement. In the negative phrase, "I am not lying, my conscience also bearing me witness in the Holy Spirit," Paul is reminding his Roman readers that his conscience is testifying by means of the Holy Spirit. It seems very possible that Paul had the Old Testament Law of Evidence in mind while using both Christ and the Holy Spirit as witnesses of his truthfulness. Deuteronomy 19:15-16 says:

> "One witness shall not rise against a man concerning any iniquity or any sin that he commits; by the mouth of two or three witnesses the matter shall be established."

Paul is saying, "If anyone questions whether or not what I'm about to speak is true, I call on both the Messiah and the Holy Spirit as witnesses of my truthfulness."

The sorrow and grief that Paul is experiencing, his heartbreak over the lost state of his "brethren in the flesh," is described as continual. The Greek word, *adialeiptos*, literally means, unceasing, without stopping. One commentator said this about Paul's burden for his people:

> "The spiritual struggle is a consuming burden, it preys upon his mind, it weighs upon his heart, his grief is incessant, it is with him day and night, he cannot escape it, it disturbs his peace and undermines his hope.His state of mind concerning his brethren after the flesh may be compared to that of a person who watches a loved one wither away and is helpless to save or provide a remedy."[1]

Paul's response to this unceasing pain in his heart over the lost state of his brethren is in the form of a wish. He writes in Romans 9:3:

> "For I could wish that I myself were accursed from Christ for my brethren, my countrymen according to the flesh,"

What is Paul saying here? Is he serious or is he speaking in hyperbole? Is there any other situation in the Bible from which Paul may be drawing?

The word "for" indicates to his readers that Paul is about to shed some light on the extent of his grief and anguish. The word translated, "I could wish," *eeuchomeen,* is used in other places of the New Testament, such as James 5:16, to clearly mean "pray." It is written in the imperfect tense, which usually means an incomplete action and in this case denotes, as Douglas Moo states, "a hypothetical nuance."[2] What Paul is saying here is that he would pray this prayer, if it were permissible and if it would benefit his lost brethren. Paul's prayer would be that he be made *anathema*, accursed from Christ. Paul is saying that he would be willing to give up his own salvation if somehow that would save his lost brethren. Since it's not possible and not permissible, the prayer never is actually prayed.

Was Paul serious? I believe Paul was so heartbroken over the lost state of his "countrymen according to the flesh" that if God would have been willing, Paul would have made the request. What Paul likely was remembering was an important event in the history of Israel involving Moses and the children of

Israel. It followed immediately after the incident with the golden calf. Exodus 32:30-32:

> Now it came to pass on the next day that Moses said to the people,"You have committed a great sin. So now I will go up to the LORD; perhaps I can make atonement for your sin." Then Moses returned to the LORD and said, "Oh, these people have committed a great sin, and have made for themselves a god of gold! Yet now, if You will forgive their sin -- but if not, I pray, blot me out of Your book which You have written."

Moses' love and willingness to sacrifice himself for the Israelites was not just familial, because they were his people. Like Paul, he was often treated badly by them as they rebelled against his leadership. Rather, it was out of his love for God, the closeness of his relationship to Him, and desiring for Israel what God desired. Moses' love for Israel was because of God's love for Israel. In the same way, Paul's love and concern for his brethren stemmed out of his love for God. If you love God and the truthfulness of His Word, you will love whom He loves. Israel, despite her disobedience of God, their rejection of Jesus as their Messiah, is still "the apple of His eye."

Paul begins verse 4 by seeking to make absolutely sure that the term "my brethren," even though modified by the phrase, "my countrymen according to the flesh," is not misunderstood to mean Christians. He says, "my brethren, my countrymen according to the flesh, who are Israelites," The term "Israelites," applies only to the nation of Israel, the physical descendants of the patriarchs, Abraham, Isaac, and Jacob. It does not mean "The Church" in any sense of the word. The late commentator, Sanford Mills, himself a Jewish believer, elaborates further on the term "Israelites":

> "The name Israel is unique, and is the name of Jacob and his descendants (Gen32:28). Exodus 4:22 applies to Jacob's descendants,"Israel is my son, my first born." Israel is an eternal nation which has never ceased, and her destiny lies in her future when she will fulfill God's purposes as His emissary."[3]

As he concludes this first section, Paul will elaborate on why he, and by application we, should grieve over the lost condition of the Jewish people. The reason is not that somehow Jewish souls have greater significance than Gentile souls. Rather, the grieving over their lost state is over the incredible blessings and privileges that were uniquely theirs, yet Israel reaped no benefit from this spiritual advantage. Paul's sorrow is over the fact that despite these incredible privileges, Israel as a nation has rejected her Messiah.

There are eight privileges uniquely given to Israel that Paul elaborates on in Romans 9:4-5:

> "who are Israelites, to whom pertain the adoption, the glory, the covenants, the giving of the law, the service of God, and the promises; of whom are the fathers and from whom, according to the flesh, Christ came, who is over all, the eternally blessed God. Amen."

The first of these eight privileges is adoption. The Greek word, *huiothesia,* literally means, the placing as a son, and likely has reference to Exodus 4:22 where the Lord says, "Israel is my son, my first born." In Hosea 11:1 as well, God says, "When Israel was a child, I loved him, And out of Egypt I called My son." Explaining this idea of adoption Steven Kreloff writes,

> "This adoption did not mean that every individual Jewish person was His child, but that Israel collectively had a special relationship with God."[4]

Moses also explained this adoption of Israel in Deuteronomy 7:6-7:

> "For you are a holy people to the LORD your God; the LORD your God has chosen you to be a people for Himself, a special treasure above all the peoples on the face of the earth."

Through this adoption Israel became the beneficiaries of God's special favor.

The second of the eight privileges is "the glory." In this context, Paul is referring to the incredible privilege the children of Israel received as they had the Shekinah glory of God, His physical presence, with them in the wilderness. Exodus 40:34-38 describes it:

> "Then the cloud covered the tabernacle of meeting, and the glory of the LORD filled the tabernacle. And Moses

was not able to enter the tabernacle of meeting, because the cloud rested above it, and the glory of the LORD filled the tabernacle. Whenever the cloud was taken up from above the tabernacle, the children of Israel would go onward in all their journeys. But if the cloud was not taken up, then they did not journey till the day that it was taken up. For the cloud of the LORD was above the tabernacle by day, and fire was over it by night, in the sight of all the house of Israel, throughout all their journeys."

Israel was unique among nations as the one who had the immeasurable privilege and blessing of having God's physical presence leading, guiding and protecting them.

The third of the privileges Paul calls "the covenants." Paul's use of the plural is unusual in that the singular is generally used more frequently. What he has in mind here is the several covenants mentioned throughout the Old Testament that God entered into with Israel, such as the Abrahamic, the Mosaic, the Davidic, and the New Covenant. Sanford Mills writes,

"These are all the eternal possessions of the nation Israel. God, who is a covenant-keeping God, is the One who deals with Israel."[5]

No other nation of people has this kind of relationship with God.

The fourth of the privileges is "the giving of the law." The law is Israel's peculiar possession. Moses reminded the people of the importance of the law in Deut 4:5-9:

"Surely I have taught you statutes and judgments, just as the LORD my God commanded me, that you should act according to them in the land which you go to possess. Therefore be careful to observe them; for this is your wisdom and your understanding in the sight of the peoples who will hear all these statutes, and say, 'Surely this great nation is a wise and understanding people.' For what great nation is there that has God so near to it, as the LORD our God is to us, for whatever reason we may call upon Him. And what great nation is there that has such statutes and righteous judgments as are in all this law which I set before you this day?"

The giving of the law was an incredible privilege to Israel and through it she was to be a means for the nations to learn about Israel's God.

The fifth of the privileges is "the service of God." The Greek word *latreia,* is used in the New Testament in the context of service or worship of God. Here Paul is likely referring to the ceremonial system, as a benefit of Israel's, that God revealed through Moses. He seems to be alluding to the sacrifices, the offerings, the various cleansings, and other means of worshiping God that were uniquely Israel's. In Ex 29:43-46, God said:

> "And there I will meet with the children of Israel, and the tabernacle shall be sanctified by My glory. So I will consecrate the tabernacle of meeting and the altar. I will also consecrate both Aaron and his sons to minister to Me as priests. I will dwell among the children of Israel and will be their God. And they shall know that I am the LORD their God, who brought them up out of the land of Egypt, that I may dwell among them. I am the LORD their God."

Israel was unique among the nations in serving the Lord in the tabernacle and in the temple.

The sixth of the privileges is "the promises." All the promises that God has made to Israel, God Himself will fulfill. He is the supreme promise keeper. Steven Kreloff writes:

> "God gave to Israel the promise of the Messiah's reign, and the promise of blessings that will flow through that reign. No other nation has ever been given these promises. All other nations receive their blessings through Israel and Israel's king."[6]

The promises of God to Israel give her a unique relationship to God among nations.

The seventh of the privileges begins Romans 9:5, where Paul writes, "of whom are the fathers." The patriarchs, Abraham, Isaac, and Jacob, and the promises of God through them, are distinctively Israel's. That is the boast of the religious leaders as they confront Jesus in John 8. Sanford Mills, quoting from the Talmud, gives insight into how important the fathers were to Israel:

> "Israel lives and endures because it supports itself on the Fathers. As the vine supports itself on the trunk which is

dry, while it, itself, is fresh and green, so Israel supports itself on the merit of the fathers, although they are already asleep. So the merit of the fathers is a general possession of the whole people of Israel, and the protection of the whole people in the day of redemption."[7] (Shemoth rabba c. 44; Beresch rabba c. 70)

The eighth and last of the privileges mentioned by Paul is that the Messiah came physically through Israel. He writes in Romans 9:5:

"and from whom, according to the flesh, Christ came, who is over all, the eternally blessed God. Amen."

Jesus The Messiah, God The Son, was born of a young Jewish virgin in Bethlehem, grew up in a Jewish home in Nazareth, and lived among His Jewish people in Israel. He was fully God and fully human, and in His humanity, He was fully Jewish. The greatest privilege that Israel had was that the Messiah was indeed one of their own. But as John sadly writes in his gospel, in John 1:11, "He came to His own, and His own did not receive Him." Paul's conclusion to this first section is a short blessing affirming the deity of the Messiah.

There has never been a nation that has been as blessed as Israel, nor has there ever been a people group that has been as blessed and as privileged as the Jewish people. But, in spite of these incredible privileges and blessings, Israel as a nation, and the Jewish people as a group, have rejected Jesus as their Messiah. This is a tragedy of eternal proportions. Without a personal relationship with their Messiah, without accepting Him as their Lord and Savior, no person, no matter how privileged and blessed, can be right with God.

Israel's failure to enter into her inheritance and to take advantage of her unique position has caused the Apostle Paul unceasing grief in his heart. This tragedy should break the heart of every believer in Jesus as well. It should also cause them to pray for the salvation of the Jewish people and ask themselves the question, "what am I doing about bringing the gospel to the people through whom Jesus came?" "Pray for the peace of Jerusalem: May they prosper who love you." (Psalm 122:6)

CHAPTER 2

The Question Of Election

In this second sermon section, Romans 9:6-13, Paul deals with the difficult subject of God's Sovereign Election. He writes in Romans 9:6,

> "But it is not that the word of God has taken no effect.
> For they are not all Israel who are of Israel,"

Paul answers an anticipated question from the previous section. Does the lack of belief among Israel mean that somehow God's Word has failed? Is God in heaven wondering why these Israelites, with all the blessings and privileges afforded them, would reject Jesus as their Messiah? The answer is absolutely not. Of course God's Word hasn't failed.

Next, to prove his point Paul introduces here the concept of the remnant, the small group of believers within physical Israel, when he writes, "For they are not all Israel who are of Israel." What does he mean when he says this? Is this talking about the church? Does this mean that only true believers, whether Jewish or Gentile, are Israel? With his statement in 9:3-4, "my brethren, my countrymen according to the flesh, who are Israelites," it is clear Paul is focusing on ethnic Israel. Douglas Moo writes:

> "Throughout these chapters, Paul carefully distinguishes between Israel and the Jews on one hand and the Gentiles on the other. Only where clear contextual pointers are present can the ethnic focus of Israel be abandoned."[8]

When Paul uses the term Israel, he is not talking about the church. So then, if this is not talking about all believers, both Jewish and Gentile, being the new spiritual Israel, what then is Paul saying here? While Paul is making a distinction between physical Israel and spiritual Israel, he is making that distinction as it relates to Israelites. Therefore, his point is that being a physical Israelite, a descendant of Abraham, Isaac, and Jacob, doesn't necessarily make one a recipient of God's blessing of salvation. The true Israel is the believing remnant within physical, ethnic Israel. Mills writes:

> "There always has been a faithful remnant in Israel. To paraphrase verse 6 of Romans 9 it would read thus, "For not all who are of Israel are Israel, there is a true Israel within the nation Israel, namely, the remnant."[9]

In the remaining part of this section, Romans 9:7-13, Paul will now support the distinction between ethnic and spiritual Israel by looking at biblical examples of God's sovereign election. He writes in Rom 9:7-9:

> "nor are they all children because they are the seed of Abraham; but, "In Isaac your seed shall be called." That is, those who are the children of the flesh, these are not the children of God; but the children of the promise are counted as the seed. For this is the word of promise: "At this time I will come and Sarah shall have a son."

In any discussion of defining Israel, one must begin where it all began, with Father Abraham. God's call of and promises to Abraham from Ur of the Chaldees is the beginning of the story of the group of people called the Hebrews. It is the basis for both physical and spiritual Israel.

The story of Abraham and his two sons is one of God's sovereign election. God promises Abraham that he would be a father of a great nation (Gen 12), and promises a son through whom the promises would flow. Abraham and Sarah decide that since Sarah was well beyond child-bearing years, they would fulfill God's promise by making a son through Sarah's Egyptian maid Hagar. Ishmael is born and Abraham desires that Ishmael would be the son of the promise. God's response is found in Gen 17:19-20:

> "Then God said: "No, Sarah your wife shall bear you a son, and you shall call his name Isaac; I will establish My covenant with him for an everlasting covenant, and with his descendants after him."

God's covenant with Abraham is sealed with the sign of circumcision, and every male in the house from Abraham through Ishmael is circumcised. Even though Ishmael has the sign of circumcision, is a physical descendant of Abraham, and is now a Hebrew, it would be Isaac through whom the promises would flow.

Paul quotes Genesis 21:12, when he says, “but in Isaac your seed shall be called.” Isaac would be the spiritual descendant of Abraham, the son of the promise, and thus the picture of spiritual Israel. He represents the believing remnant. Paul used the establishment of the nation to show that God’s method of dealing with Israel has always been by sovereign election. By choosing Isaac over Ishmael, God established a pattern of election that continues to this day. Paul continues the discussion in Romans 9:10-13:

> And not only this, but when Rebekah also had conceived by one man, even by our father Isaac (for the children not yet being born, nor having done any good or evil, that the purpose of God according to election might stand, not of works but of Him who calls), it was said to her, "The older shall serve the younger." As it is written, "Jacob I have loved, but Esau I have hated."

The transitional phrase, “and not only this,” makes it clear that what follows takes the argument to the next level.

We can say that the reasons for God’s choice of Isaac over Ishmael were pretty self-evident. Abraham and Sarah did not obey God by using Hagar as a surrogate, and through their disobedience the child Ishmael was born. This was never God’s intent and that is explained when God says to Abraham, “but, In Isaac your seed shall be called." But why did God choose Jacob over Esau?

As Paul begins his line of reasoning, he deals first of all with the thought that perhaps it was because Jacob’s heart was more directed toward God, his character more righteous than Esau. He shows the fallacy of this by stating that this took place prior to their birth, prior to their having done neither good nor evil. So what is the reason for God’s choosing Jacob? The sole reason for God choosing Jacob over Esau was election. It was God’s plan to choose Jacob, and so therefore, he chose Jacob. Moo writes:

> “Isaac was chosen; Ishmael was not. Jacob was chosen; Esau was not. By these choices God has seen to it that his plan to bring into existence a people who would be his “peculiar possession” would remain.”[10]

God purposed in his heart to bring this to pass and he brought it to pass. That's what Paul is alluding to when he says, in Rom 9:11, "that the purpose of God according to election might stand, not of works but of Him who calls." Election rests in the sovereignty of God. Paul concludes his argument with two Old Testament quotes in Rom 9:12-13:

> it was said to her, "The older shall serve the younger."
> As it is written, "Jacob I have loved, but Esau I have hated."

The entire promise given to Rebekah is found in Gen 25:23 and gives further illumination into what God meant:

> "And the LORD said to her: "two nations are in your womb, two peoples shall be separated from your body; one people shall be stronger than the other, And the older shall serve the younger."

Because there is no biblical record of Esau ever serving Jacob, the key words to note in this passage are the words "nations" and "peoples." The nation that was descended from Esau was known as Edom and the people called Edomites. In judgment God made the idolatrous Edomites, who came from Esau, servants to the Israelites, who came from Jacob. This prophecy given to Rebekah was fulfilled in the time of David (2 Sam 8:14).

The point to Paul's argument is that God's election is His. He chooses whom He chooses and it will often be contrary to human law and here in the Old Testament, Jewish custom. Mills explains this when he writes:

> "The declaration in verse 12 ("the older shall serve the younger") is contrary to law and Jewish custom. The older son was always the accepted heir who received the greater portion of his father's estate. God chooses the very opposite of that which man chooses, and has always done so. God did not choose Abraham's Ishmael, but Abraham's Isaac. He did not choose Isaac's Esau, but Isaac's Jacob. He did not choose Jacob's eldest son Reuben, but Jacob's fourth son Judah. He did not choose Jesse' first born son Eliab, but Jesse's youngest son David. In all these instances God's choice was contrary to human law and Jewish custom. God's action and election are always according to His own will."[11]

The second of the two Old Testament quotes in Rom 9:12-13, "Jacob I have loved, but Esau I have hated," has been a little more difficult to explain.

The quote that Paul uses here is taken from Malachi 1:2-3 and is presented in the context of how God has loved Israel:

> "I have loved you," says the LORD. "Yet you say, 'In what way have You loved us?' Was not Esau Jacob's brother?" Says the LORD, "Yet Jacob I have loved; But Esau I have hated, And laid waste his mountains and his heritage for the jackals of the wilderness."

Clearly God is not referring to individuals. He's not talking about loving Jacob nor Esau personally. He is, in the context of both the Romans 9:13 quote and the Malachi 1:2-3 quote, referring to them as nations. As Steven Kreloff writes:

> "God was saying at the beginning of Israel's history He chose Jacob over Esau before they were born, and at the close of Israel's Old Testament history He could sum up His attitude toward His chosen people as love and His attitude toward the idolatrous nation of Edom as hate."[12]

The difficulty in this verse is the negative understanding of the word "hate." It's just not something that people want to attribute to God. Therefore, what some commentators do is point to what Jesus said about discipleship in Luke 14:26, and how the word "hate" was used. Jesus said:

> "If anyone comes to Me and does not hate his father and mother, wife and children, brothers and sisters, yes, and his own life also, he cannot be My disciple"

Obviously Jesus isn't advocating people hate their parents, their spouses, their children, their families and their own lives. Instead, in the context of discipleship, a disciple's love for God will be so intense and strong that in comparison, love for parents will appear like hate. In the same way then, what Paul is saying is that God's love for Jacob is so strong that in comparison, His love for Esau appears like hatred.

This position does not take into account the complete context of the Malachi portion. Following God's statement, "Yet Jacob I have loved; But Esau I have hated, He continues by saying:

> "and laid waste his mountains and his heritage for the jackals of the wilderness." Even though Edom has said, "We have been impoverished, But we will return and build the desolate places," Thus says the LORD of hosts: "They may build, but I will throw down; They shall be called the Territory of Wickedness, And the people against whom the LORD will have indignation forever." (Malachi 1:3-4)

God states that He will have indignation against Edom forever. In other words, God's hatred for Esau's descendants the Edomites is eternal and is active forever. It is a matter of His sovereign election, His choice. To make it mean anything other than what it says blurs the Scriptures, especially regarding the concept of election. Sanford Mills rightly concludes regarding this concept of God's love of Jacob and hatred of Esau:

> "The unmistakable and unchanging expression of God's hate toward the descendants of Esau must be understood to be toward them as a nation, not as individuals. We must never lose sight of the truth that the grace of God is still able to grant eternal life to the individual descendant of Esau. By the same token, we must never lose sight of the truth that every Jew who rejects Jesus Christ is lost and doomed to a sinner's hell forever."[13]

The illustrations of Isaac and Jacob give us a wonderful picture of God's sovereign election of Israel. The history of Israel is marked by an elect remnant not chosen on the basis of personal merit or physical descent but by divine calling. It is this remnant of Jewish believers that Paul is speaking about when he says, "For they are not all Israel who are of Israel." Only this remnant is the true Israel through whom God will fulfill His promises made to the patriarchs.

CHAPTER 3

Is There Unrighteousness With God?

Having looked specifically at Israel in the beginning of Chapter 9, in the next sermon section Paul takes a bit of a detour. He stops his teaching on Israel for a moment and states a rhetorical question, addressing whether God's election is unjust. He writes in Romans 9:14:

> "What shall we say then? Is there unrighteousness with God? Certainly not!"

Though this was a particular style of teaching that Paul used, with rhetorical questions and answers, the question of whether God's sovereign election is righteous or just was likely heard by Paul in the course of his ministry and would be on the minds of some of Paul's listeners.

Before Paul goes ahead and answers the rhetorical questions using illustrations from the Scriptures, he makes absolutely clear his own position on the question. His response in the Greek, *meé génoito,* is the strongest possible negative, translated in different versions, "certainly not," "God forbid," "by no means," "not at all," "may it never be." He uses this phrase throughout the book of Romans and will use it two other times in Romans 11.

Paul's first illustration to demonstrate why he felt so strongly on this issue is taken from Exodus 33. He writes in Romans 9:15:

> "For He says to Moses, "I will have mercy on whomever I will have mercy, and I will have compassion on whomever I will have compassion."

This is a quote from Exodus 33:19 and takes place following God's judging the children of Israel after the incident of the golden calf. God judged the children of Israel and three thousand died as a result of this judgment, but God spared the nation. God says to Moses in Exodus 33:17-19:

> "I will also do this thing that you have spoken; for you have found grace in My sight, and I know you by name."

> And he said, "Please, show me Your glory." Then He said, "I will make all My goodness pass before you, and I will proclaim the name of the LORD before you. I will be gracious to whom I will be gracious, and I will have compassion on whom I will have compassion."

God's message to Moses was that while Israel deserved to die because of their horrible sin against God, nevertheless, because He is a compassionate God, Israel was spared and survived. Israel owed her very survival as a nation to the compassionate and gracious election of God.

Paul uses this illustration of God graciously sparing the Israelites following the golden calf incident to answer the charge that God's choosing of some for salvation is not just. "What shall we say then? Is there unrighteousness with God? Certainly not!" If a person thinks that God electing some and not others is unjust, then they logically should conclude that God sparing Israel after the golden calf was also unjust.

The problem with people's logic has to do with their understanding of what fallen people deserve from God. On the one hand, if one believes that God chooses some to judgment and others to salvation then one can logically question the basis of that choice by God. On the other hand, if one believes, as the Bible teaches, that all of us are born sinful and condemned before a holy God (Romans 3:23; 5:12,18; Psalm 51:5), and deserve judgment, then election, instead of being unjust, is merciful. Everyone deserves God's judgment and wrath, but those elected to salvation receive the amazing grace and mercy of God. God would be absolutely just if He never chose anyone to experience salvation.

Paul concludes the first part of this section with a statement in Rom 9:16:

> "So then it is not of him who wills, nor of him who runs, but of God who shows mercy."

The phrase in the Greek, *ára oún*, translated, so then, is used exclusively by Paul in the New Testament and introduces a conclusion. The conclusion by Paul is that God's choice is not based upon the person who wants to receive mercy the most ("him who wills"), nor based upon the person who puts the most effort into receiving mercy ("him who runs"). God's choice is based solely on God's choice ("of God who shows mercy"). "I will be gracious to whom I will be gracious, and I will have compassion on whom I will have compassion."

The second part of this section is an additional argument from the book of Exodus. Paul quotes Exodus 9:16 in Romans 9:17:

> "For the Scripture says to the Pharaoh, "For this very purpose I have raised you up, that I may show My power in you, and that My name may be declared in all the earth."

The context for this quote from Exodus 9:16 is best understood by looking at an earlier portion from Exodus 4:21-22:

> And the LORD said to Moses, "When you go back to Egypt, see that you do all those wonders before Pharaoh which I have put in your hand. But I will harden his heart, so that he will not let the people go."

Even before Moses was aware of all the details of what would be taking place in Egypt, God revealed the fact that He would harden Pharaoh's heart in order to bring glory to Himself. This would happen prior to the exodus itself from Egypt resulting in the plagues, culminating in the death of the firstborn of Egypt, and again at the parting of the Red Sea, through the drowning of Pharaoh's army.

The question that this raises, which Paul is addressing, again has to do with whether God was unjust. Was it just for God to harden Pharaoh's heart? Certainly, there are a number of Scriptures that say Pharaoh hardened his own heart. Exodus 7:13-14 is one example of this:

> "And Pharaoh's heart grew hard, and he did not heed them, as the LORD had said. So the LORD said to Moses: "Pharaoh's heart is hard; he refuses to let the people go."

Clearly, God did not do anything that forced Pharaoh to act contrary to his natural inclinations. However, the Scriptures also make it clear that God hardened Pharaoh's heart as a means of accomplishing His will. H.L. Ellison writes:

> "We may fairly deduce from this that God did not choose and raise up a Pharaoh who was compelled to act contrary

> to his natural character. At the same time the priority given to God's declaration of coming hardening cannot fairly be interpreted as meaning God's punishment for man's self-willed hardening, which he foreknew. However much human cooperation there may have been, the hardening was part of God's express purpose, not for the Pharaoh's ruin – we are given no hint as to his eternal destiny – but for the carrying through of God's purposes."[14]

God was not unjust for hardening Pharaoh's heart, nor was He unjust for withholding mercy from Pharaoh. The Scriptures reveal that God indeed accomplished His purposes through Pharaoh as the Passover story proclaims year after year. Ultimately, God doing what He wills to do is not something new, nor something that only applies to the Israelites of Paul's day, or of today. God has always acted according to His own wisdom and purpose. The Old Testament events Paul used as illustrations bear this out. That's what Paul's conclusion is in Rom 9:18, "Therefore He has mercy on whom He wills, and whom He wills He hardens."

The implications of this on evangelism are obvious. Sanford Mills rightly concludes by writing:

> "The doctrine of the Sovereignty of God is the greatest incentive to preaching the Gospel. Since no one knows who will accept, it is imperative that the Gospel be proclaimed everywhere and at all times, to all classes of people."[15]

Having dealt with the question of the justice of God's sovereign choosing of some for salvation, in the next section Paul anticipated a second and more pronounced objection, the objection that God's election would somehow negate man's responsibility. He writes in Romans 9:19:

> "You will say to me then, "Why does He still find fault? For who has resisted His will?"

When asked how he reconciled the doctrines of divine election vs. human responsibility, Charles Haddon Spurgeon responded, "I don't, for I never try reconciling friends."[16] Unfortunately, the question of God's election vs. human responsibility has been a point of division in the church for many centuries. Rather than seeing the two doctrines as friends, they are seen as mortal enemies, doctrines which are mutually exclusive.

At first glance the question appears to be an honest inquiry regarding the validity of human responsibility in light of God's election. How can God still find fault with people who resist Him if only those whom He chooses will be saved? Isn't that unjust? Douglas Moo writes:

> "Before analyzing what Paul does say in response to this objection, we do well to note what he does *not* say. He makes no reference to human works or human faith (whether foreseen or not) as the basis for God's act of hardening (as so many of Paul's "defenders" have done). Nor does he defuse the issue by confining God's hardening only to matters of salvation history; quite the contrary, vv 22-23 make more explicit than ever that Paul is dealing with questions of eternal destiny. Paul is content to hold the truths of God's absolute sovereignty – in both election and in hardening – and of full human responsibility with out reconciling them. [17]

Paul, just as Spurgeon stated, never tried to reconcile the friends of divine election and human responsibility. Instead, Paul centers his attention on the real issue at hand. People who question the justice of God, electing some while holding others accountable for their unbelief, simply don't understand God. Paul spends the next few verses putting the issue in its proper perspective. He writes in Rom 9:20-21:

> "But indeed, O man, who are you to reply against God? Will the thing formed say to him who formed it, "Why have you made me like this?" Does not the potter have power over the clay, from the same lump to make one vessel for honor and another for dishonor?"

Paul turns the tables and questions the one who would question God's righteousness and justice. The Amplified Bible captures the impatience and exasperation in Paul's voice in Romans 9:20:

> "But who are you, a mere man, to criticize and contradict and answer back to God?"

Paul doesn't treat this question as an honest inquiry, but rather as an evil accusation against God's character. The imagery that he uses to teach a lesson to this person making the accusation is a very common Old Testament illustration, that of the potter and the clay. What Paul states in Romans 9:20-21 is a quote from Isaiah 29:16:

> "Will the thing formed say to him who formed it, "Why have you made me like this?" Does not the potter have power over the clay, from the same lump to make one vessel for honor and another for dishonor?"

How ridiculous would it be for a piece of clay to complain about how it was made or what form it took. That is the line of reasoning that Paul is using here. Doesn't the potter have a right to mold the clay into whatever form he chooses? In the same way God can do whatever He pleases with man. It is important to note that Paul is not referring to the potter here as creator. He is not asking whether the one creating has a right to create as he pleases. Steven Kreloff states why the distinction is important:

> "The Bible does not teach that God originally created man sinful and that He has a right to create sinful creatures in order to punish them. Adam was created in a state of innocence and chose to sin. The force of Paul's argument is that God is like a potter working with clay. A potter does not create clay; he takes the clay as he finds it. While God knew man would sin, He did not create him sinful. God is not responsible for man's sin. God has simply taken the lump of clay known as sinful humanity and by sovereign election fashioned some of the clay into vessels that receive mercy.[18]

Paul continues the discussion with another question beginning in Rom 9:22-24:

> "What if God, wanting to show His wrath and to make His power known, endured with much longsuffering the vessels of wrath prepared for destruction, and that He might make known the riches of His glory on the vessels of mercy, which He had prepared beforehand for glory, even us whom He called, not of the Jews only, but also of the Gentiles?"

In order to understand what Paul is trying to teach in this portion we must look carefully at these two groups of people called "vessels of wrath" and "vessels of mercy." The "vessels of wrath" are said to be "prepared for destruction," while of the "vessels of mercy" it is said that "He had prepared beforehand for glory." The difference is significant. In the first word, the Greek *kateertisména,* translated prepared, is a middle/passive participle that does not clearly bring God into the picture. In the second word, the Greek *proeetoímasen,* translated "He had prepared beforehand" is an active participle and clearly God is seen as the one doing the preparing. As John Stott states:

> "Certainly God has never 'prepared' anybody for destruction; is it not that by their own evildoing they prepare themselves for it?"[19]

The question must be asked then, for what purpose has God "endured with much longsuffering the vessels of wrath prepared for destruction?" Clearly, 9:23 gives the primary purpose, "that He might make known the riches of His glory on the vessels of mercy." I believe this primary purpose of God's longsuffering has to do with keeping the window of opportunity open for as long as possible so that some, "vessels of wrath prepared for destruction," might eventually become "vessels of mercy which He had prepared beforehand for glory." Paul had already taught this concept earlier in Romans 2:4-6:

> "Or do you despise the riches of His goodness, forbearance, and longsuffering, not knowing that the goodness of God leads you to repentance? But in accordance with your hardness and your impenitent heart you are treasuring up for yourself wrath in the day of wrath and revelation of the righteous judgment of God, who "will render to each one according to his deeds."

That those addressed as "vessels of wrath" could become "vessels of mercy" is not unprecedented in the Scriptures. Paul addresses believers in Ephesus by saying to them in Eph 2:1-3:

> "And you He made alive, who were dead in trespasses and sins, in which you once walked according to the course of this world, according to the prince of the power of the air, the spirit who now works in the sons of

disobedience, among whom also we all once conducted ourselves in the lusts of our flesh, fulfilling the desires of the flesh and of the mind, and were by nature children of wrath, just as the others."

Without repentance, without coming to faith in Christ, these believers would have remained as children or vessels of wrath.

The two other purposes given in Romans 9:22, "wanting to show His wrath and to make His power known," must be understood in relation to the primary purpose. Cranfield writes:

"God has endured a Pharaoh, and He now endures rebellious Israel, with much long-suffering for the sake of the manifestation of the riches of His glory on the vessels of mercy, and also for the sake of the revelation of His wrath, and of His power, (His saving power), since this twofold revelation is necessary for the achievement of His ultimate purpose of manifesting the riches of His glory. It is that the relations between God's patient enduring of vessels of wrath, the showing of His wrath, and the manifestation of the wealth of His glory upon vessels of mercy, will be illuminated by 9:30-11:36."[20]

In other words, since Paul here is addressing the question of Israel's rejection of Jesus as their Messiah, we shall see that the ultimate purpose in God's long-suffering toward a rebellious Israel is for them to repent and ultimately return to Him, which will manifest the riches of His glory. Paul will show that in the process of that happening God will also reveal His wrath and His saving power.

Paul concludes this section by first emphasizing that the "vessels of mercy" were both Jews and Gentiles and then affirms and illustrates that statement with some Old Testament quotations from Hosea and Isaiah. He writes in Rom 9:23-29:

"and that He might make known the riches of His glory on the vessels of mercy, which He had prepared beforehand for glory, even us whom He called, not of the Jews only, but also of the Gentiles? As He says also in Hosea: "I will call them My people, who were not My people, And her beloved, who was not beloved." "And it shall come to pass in the place where it was said to them,' You are not My people,' There they shall be

> called sons of the living God." Isaiah also cries out concerning Israel: "Though the number of the children of Israel be as the sand of the sea, The remnant will be saved. For He will finish the work and cut it short in righteousness, Because the LORD will make a short work upon the earth."And as Isaiah said before: "Unless the LORD of Sabaoth had left us a seed,We would have become like Sodom, And we would have been made like Gomorrah."

Paul's first Old Testament quote is from Hosea 2:23 and 1:10. The Hosea portions, though describing the lost people of Israel specifically, are used in application by Paul to emphasize the inclusion of Gentiles in the Body of Christ as "vessels of mercy." Peter, in a similar way in 1 Peter 2:10, also uses this portion in Hosea to apply to Gentiles. The important point to note here is that this doesn't show that the "Church" has replaced Israel, but on the contrary shows that the promises given to Israel by God are to be fulfilled literally, despite that application of the passage to the Gentiles. Mills states:

> "There are numerous ways in which a text can be applied. But there is only one true interpretation and implication. The apostles Paul and Peter are applying the passage in Hosea to the New Testament saint. They do not negate its true meaning. Hosea 2:23 promises Israel's restoration to their 'peoplehood' and to their land before the millennium. Romans 9:25 places the saint on the same basis as God places Israel. Israel is God's eternal earthly people, and the born-again believers are God's heavenly people."[21]

The use of the phrase "the place" in Hosea 1:10 is a clear prophecy of the restoration of the land to the people of Israel, where they again will indeed be called "sons of the living God."

In Romans 9:27-28, Paul quotes from Isaiah 10:22-23 which says:

> "For though your people, O Israel, be as the sand of the sea, a remnant of them will return; the destruction decreed shall overflow with righteousness. For the Lord GOD of hosts will make a determined end in the midst of all the land."

Here, Paul makes clear reference to the remnant of Israel who will be the true believers from among the physical descendants of Abraham, Isaac, and Jacob. God, in His sovereign choice and calling, will always preserve a remnant for Himself. This was true during the time of Isaiah and through the Babylonian captivity. It was true during the first coming of Jesus, as the majority of Israel rejected Him as their King Messiah, but yet there was still a sizable minority of Jewish believers who constituted the early church. It is true today as Jewish believers, part of the Body of Christ, are called by Paul in Romans 11:5 "a remnant according to the election of grace." And it will also be true in the future when during the "end times," there will also be a remnant who will believe in Jesus' return as their Messiah during the "Great Tribulation".

Romans 9:28 has the "end times" in mind when Paul writes:

> "For He will finish the work and cut it short in righteousness, because the LORD will make a short work upon the earth."

The verse that gives detail to this statement is Matthew 24:21-22,

> "For then there will be great tribulation, such as has not been since the beginning of the world until this time, no, nor ever shall be. And unless those days were shortened, no flesh would be saved; but for the elect's sake those days will be shortened."

Unless God intervenes and cuts short the devastation of the tribulation period, man would destroy himself. Without anyone saved from this destruction and wrath of God to come, then the earthly kingdom of Messiah, promised to David in 2 Samuel 7 could not be established in Jerusalem.

In Romans 9:29, Paul concludes this section with a quote from Isaiah 1:9:

> "And as Isaiah said before: "Unless the LORD of Sabaoth had left us a seed, we would have become like Sodom, and we would have been made like Gomorrah."

This final quote emphasizes God's grace in sparing this remnant of Israel, this seed. While God's perfect righteousness requires Him to deal with Israel's sin and rebellion, His love for Israel, His grace and mercy will not allow her to experience the same annihilation experienced by Sodom and Gomorrah. As Douglas Moo writes, "this concluding note of hope for this section paves the way for Romans 11."[22]

One of the reasons Romans 9 through 11 is so important is that it substantiates for all believers God's trustworthiness to Israel and to all of His saints. If God couldn't keep the promises He made to Abraham and his descendants, promises of a perpetual people, a promised land for His people, and a king on the throne of David, then why should we believe anything He has promised in the Scriptures for us? But God has kept His promises, they will all be fulfilled, and we can trust Him for our eternal souls. He truly is the one and only "Promise Keeper".

CHAPTER 4

What Shall We Say Then?

As we come to the final sermon section of Romans 9, Paul concludes his previous thoughts by drawing us a picture of the current unbelief of the vast majority of Israel, which continues into chapter 10, and makes comparison to Gentile believers in Jesus. He writes in Romans 9:30-31,

> "What shall we say then? That Gentiles, who did not pursue righteousness, have attained to righteousness, even the righteousness of faith; but Israel, pursuing the law of righteousness, has not attained to the law of righteousness."

With the question, "What shall we say then?" Paul is asking, in light of the arguments that I have already laid out for you, what legitimate conclusions can we make here?

In this portion Paul moves from divine sovereignty to human responsibility. He presents for us a situation that is paradoxical, completely topsy-turvy, where everything is upside-down. One might, from a human perspective, even call this bizarre. Nothing seems to be the way it's supposed to be. This reminds me of the Bizarro World in Superman comics. This was a parallel universe, a mirror world of earth, where everything and everyone were an opposite of what they were supposed to be. Bizarro Superman was a villain instead of a hero. Bizarro Lex Luthor was the hero instead of a villain. The planet was square instead of round. Ugly was beautiful and beautiful was ugly. It was just a very bizarre place. So, too, with the picture of what Paul is showing us in Rom 9:30-31:

> "Gentiles, who did not pursue righteousness, have attained to righteousness, even the righteousness of faith; but Israel, pursuing the law of righteousness, has not attained to the law of righteousness."

The first people group that Paul mentions here are the Gentiles, and he says that they "did not pursue righteousness." Paul had met and known many Gentiles, among whom were likely people with high moral character and upright citizens of Rome. So logically he is not speaking of moral righteousness, but rather the righteousness that brings a right standing with God. How then did Gentiles attain to this status when they were not even seeking it?

First, as Paul explains, the righteousness that the Gentiles attained is a righteousness "that comes by faith." And faith, as Paul has already made clear in Romans 1:16-17, is a response that any person, Jew or Gentile, can make. Second, the Gentiles attaining righteousness are an important example of a principle that he has already taught in Romans 9:16, "it is not of him who wills, nor of him who runs, but of God who shows mercy." This faith is from God, a gift, as Paul also taught in Ephesians 2:8:

> "For by grace you have been saved through faith, and
> that not of yourselves; it is the gift of God,"

The second people group that Paul mentions here is Israel, the Jewish people, and of them he says in Romans 9:31-33:

> "but Israel, pursuing the law of righteousness,
> has not attained to the law of righteousness. Why?
> Because they did not seek it by faith, but as it were,
> by the works of the law. For they stumbled at that
> stumbling stone. As it is written: "Behold, I lay in
> Zion a stumbling stone and rock of offense, And
> whoever believes on Him will not be put to shame."

The idea of pursuing the law of righteousness, as Paul describes it here, is a continuous seeking after what's promised in the Law of Moses which is what the Greek word for law, *nómon* is referring to. Israel was constantly seeking to attain to a righteousness which required that the law be kept perfectly. Moo writes:

> "Israel should have realized that the law could never
> be truly reached through works; that human sin would
> always prevent its promise to justify those who do it
> from being fulfilled.[23]

Paul uses a different Greek word for "attained" here in v. 31 than he used in v. 30. The word "attained" in v. 30, *katelaben,* literally means to "lay hold of so as to make one's own." The word "attained" in v. 31, *éfthasen* means to "arrive at" or "reach"

The difference in the two words makes clear what Paul continues to say in v. 32. The reason Israel did not arrive at the goal was, "Because they did not seek it by faith, but as it were, by the works of the law."

Israel did not confess regarding their inability to keep the Law perfectly and turn by faith to God for forgiveness. Instead they kept trying to keep the Law by their own efforts. It proved to be futile. Consequently, they stumbled over the "stumbling Stone." The Lord Jesus The Messiah did not measure up to Israel's expectations, so they rejected Him, instead of responding to Him by faith. Paul, quoting from Isaiah 8:14 and 28:16, demonstrates how God understood what would be the two differing reactions by men to the "Stone that God layed in Zion." It would be "a stumbling stone" and "rock of offense."

The Greek word translated "stumbling stone," *Líthon proskómmatos,* paints a picture of a rock in the road causing someone to trip and fall over it. Paul uses it in that way in 1 Corinthians 8:9, when talking about the liberty of God's grace:

> "But beware lest somehow this liberty of yours become a stumbling block to those who are weak."

The vast majority of Israel, the Jewish people, intent on trying to be righteous enough to be right with God by keeping the law, stumble over the reality of salvation by grace alone, through faith alone, in Christ alone.

The Greek word translated "rock of offence," *petran skandalou,* describes what the cross has become to the Jewish people. The cross has become a scandal. Sanford Mills, understanding the Jewish mindset writes:

> "To Israel, Christ and all His accomplishments on the cross, His Resurrection, His Ascension, and His Return, are nothing less than a scandal. Christ, say the Jews today, has become the Gentile's God. His coming on the world's horizon, and that which people have made of Him are, to Israel, disgraceful, shocking, outrageous, and iniquitous. All of these implications are contained in the Greek word *skandalon.*"[24]

The history of the church toward the Jewish people has been marked often, unfortunately, by anti-semitism and hatred. One of the great "Church Fathers," John Chrysostom, known as the "golden throat" for his great sermons, preached this hateful diatribe:

> "Jews are the most worthless of men – they are lecherous, greedy, rapacious… they worship the devil. It is incumbent on all Christians to hate Jews" (Homily 1:3-64:1)

Some of my own personal experiences growing up, especially being called "Christ Killer" as a youngster, caused me to believe that Christianity was anti-Semitic. This is not an uncommon belief among Jewish people. If there is going to be effective evangelism among the Jewish people, the church must recognize, as Paul clearly teaches here at the end of Romans 9, that to the Jewish people, the Gospel of Jesus Christ is a "rock of offence," a scandal. There is much we have to overcome.

John Stott in summarizing Romans 9 writes:

> "Paul began this chapter with the paradox of Israel's privilege and prejudice (1-5). How can her unbelief be explained? It is not because God is unfaithful to His promises, for He has kept His word in relation to the Israel within Israel (6-13). It is not because God is unjust in His 'purpose according to election', for neither His mercy on some nor His hardening of others is incompatible with His justice (14-18). It is not because God is unfair to blame Israel or to hold human beings accountable, for we should not answer Him back, and in any case He has acted according to His own character and according to Old Testament prophecy (19-29). It is rather because Israel is proud, pursuing righteousness in the wrong way, by works instead of faith, and so has stumbled over the stumbling-block of the cross (30-33). Thus this chapter about Israel's unbelief begins with God's purpose of election (6-29) and concludes by attributing Israel's fall to her own pride (30-33)."[25]

CHAPTER 5

A Prayerful Heart For Israel's Salvation

Romans 10:1 begins the next sermon section. Paul begins Romans 10 in much the same way he began Romans 9, by sharing with his readers his heart regarding Israel. He writes in Rom 10:1:

> "Brethren, my heart's desire and prayer to God for Israel is that they may be saved."

Having spent the beginning of Romans 9 sharing his "great sorrow and continual grief" in his heart over the plight of his brethren, his "countrymen according to the flesh," and describing the reason for their lost state at the latter part of the chapter, Paul now shares his response to their lostness. In essence Paul says, now that I've shown you that they are lost apart from Christ, you need to know that my most heartfelt prayer for them is for their salvation. J.B. Phillips' paraphrase captures the intensity of Paul's plea to God:

> "My brothers, from the bottom of my heart I long and pray to God that Israel may be saved."

The fact that Paul continued to pray so earnestly for the salvation of Israel, the unbelieving Jewish people, clearly shows that he did not believe their present rejection of Jesus as final or complete.

The response of Paul, the apostle to the Gentiles, to the lostness of the Jewish people, was heartfelt prayer and evangelistic fervor. He never stopped praying for their salvation nor stopped sharing the gospel with them until he breathed his last breath. That is a wonderful example to all believers, not just Jewish believers, on what our response ought to be regarding the lostness of the Jewish people. We should be praying for their salvation and, where God gives opportunity, sharing the gospel with them.

Romans 10:1 is a clear contradiction to the heresy that has found some favor in the evangelical church called the "Two Covenant Theory." This theory states that Jewish people do not have to accept Jesus as their Messiah and Savior in order to be right with God but rather are saved through the covenants God made with the Jewish people in the Old Testament, beginning with the Abrahamic covenant. In essence only Gentiles need to believe in Jesus in order to be saved; hence two covenants. Would Paul have "great sorrow and unceasing grief in his heart" if he thought that Jewish people were saved apart from Christ, from their Messiah? Would his "heart's desire and prayer to God for Israel be that they may be saved," if he didn't believe they were lost apart from Jesus? Obviously, the answer is no.

Beginning in Romans 10:2, Paul testifies to why they are lost apart from Jesus:

> "For I bear them witness that they have a zeal for God,
> but not according to knowledge."

Having been one of those of whom he refers to here, Paul can accurately say as the NIV translates, "For I can testify about them." From his own personal experiences as Saul, the Pharisee of Pharisees, Paul knows what he's talking about when he says, "they have a zeal for God." Describing that zeal Mills writes:

> "What other apostle is better qualified to bear more convincing testimony to Israel's zeal than Paul? It was his zeal, both before and after his conversion, that consumed his time, his mind, his heart, and his soul. It was Paul's passionate zeal as a Pharisee when he caused Jewish Christians to be killed. He counted himself blameless as touching the righteousness which is in the Law, and he thought he was doing God's will in fulfilling the very letter of the Law. How blind was Paul before his conversion!"[26]

The word zeal means to have a fervent or enthusiastic devotion, often extreme or fanatical in nature, as to a religious movement, political cause, ideal, or aspiration. That certainly describes the history of the Jewish people, fervent devotion to God. The Greek word translated zeal is *zeélon,* and it is from the root word meaning to boil over with heat. The fervent devotion, as Paul remembered, virtually boiled over with passion. When Jesus charged the church at Laodicea with being lukewarm, in essence he was saying they had lost their zeal for Him.

This zeal, Paul says, is "not according to knowledge." The Greek word translated knowledge, *epígnoosin,* defines "exact or full knowledge, discernment, or recognition." Steven Kreloff describes this zeal that is not according to knowledge:

> "Israel was religiously fanatic, but their zeal wasn't based on a full understanding of the Hebrew Scriptures. Although they were familiar with God's Word, they misunderstood the intention of His law. They believed they could establish their own righteousness by obeying the numerous biblical commands. Their zeal for good works stemmed from an ardent attempt to be in right relation to God." [27]

In late 2002, I had the privilege of visiting Israel for the first time. One of the most moving experiences that I, as a Jewish believer had, was praying at the Wailing Wall. While I was praying at the wall, I became aware of the presence of two Orthodox Jewish men praying on both sides of me. As these two men were davening, praying and bowing at the mention of God's name, according to Jewish tradition, I was overcome with emotion, as God brought Romans 10:1-2 to my heart and mind. I could identify with Paul's broken heart, as I thought of his words and began to weep:

> "Brethren, my heart's desire and prayer to God for Israel is that they may be saved. For I bear them witness that they have a zeal for God, but not according to knowledge."

How zealous these two men were for God! Yet no matter how much they prayed and how hard they bowed before God, they could never be made righteous apart from the Messiah, whom they simply did not know.

Paul continued his discussion of Israel's lostness in Romans 10:3:

> "For they being ignorant of God's righteousness, and seeking to establish their own righteousness, have not submitted to the righteousness of God."

Paul says Israel is ignorant of, they fail to understand or recognize, God's mode of righteousness. From the very beginning of their Hebrew Scriptures, God's mode of righteousness was made known. When Adam and Eve ate from the tree of the knowledge of good and evil, they understood that they had sinned and that their relationship with God was fractured. They tried to cover their sin with fig leaves, God covered their sin with animal skins. There was a death, shed blood that paid the price for those sins.

The Levitical sacrifices continued that practice under the Law. Leviticus 17:11 says:

> "For the life of the flesh is in the blood, and I have given it to you upon the altar to make atonement for your souls; for it is the blood that makes atonement for the soul."

Every time a Jewish person participated in the sacrificial system they should have been reminded that "it is the blood that makes atonement for the soul." When John the Baptist saw Jesus and said in John 1:29, "Behold! The Lamb of God who takes away the sin of the world," those who believed in Him recognized Him as God's provision for their need of righteousness. This wasn't some new teaching on God's righteousness. Yet, Israel struggled and stumbled over it, and the majority were ignorant of it.

Because they were ignorant of God's mode of righteousness, they misunderstood the purpose and goal of the law and attempted to reach God through their own self-conceived works of righteousness, as Paul wrote in Rom 10:3:

> "seeking to establish their own righteousness, have not submitted to the righteousness of God."

They had their eyes focused on themselves rather than on the Bible, and they created a perceived means for establishing and attaining righteousness. Rather than submitting to God's mode of righteousness, faith in Jesus the Messiah, they created their own, man-made way, which contradicted their own Hebrew Scriptures. Paul describes his own life as he came to understand God's righteousness in Phil 3:7-9:

> "But what things were gain to me, these I have counted loss for Christ. Yet indeed I also count all things loss for the excellence of the knowledge of Christ Jesus my Lord, for whom I have suffered the loss of all things, and count them as rubbish, that I may gain Christ and be found in Him, not having my own righteousness, which is from

> the law, but that which is through faith in Christ, the righteousness which is from God by faith;"

Keeping the Law, doing the works of the Law, was never God's way of attaining to righteousness. No one understood that better than Paul as he remembered back on his days as the Pharisee Saul.

In Romans 10:4, Paul makes a very important statement regarding the Law and righteousness. He writes:

> "For Christ is the end of the law for righteousness to everyone who believes."

To understand fully what Paul is saying here, the meaning of the Greek word *télos*, translated "end," must be determined, as well as the Greek word *nómou,* translated "law."

Bible scholars have argued for four different meanings to the word translated "law." They say it either means, (1) law in general, in whatever form; (2) Old Testament revelation; (3) legalism; or (4) the Mosaic law. Of the four meanings argued, I would concur with the vast majority who say it is referring to the Mosaic law. That meaning clearly fits with the context of what Paul is saying here. So the question still to be answered is, "What does Paul mean when he says, 'For Christ is the end of the Mosaic law?'"

There are two main schools of thought as to what Paul means when he says Christ is the "end of the law." One would say that "end" should be understood to mean "goal." Cranfield in support of this position writes:

> "At this point a statement that Christ is the goal to which all along the law has been directed, its true intention and meaning, is altogether apposite. Israel has misunderstood the law, because it failed to recognize what it was all about. Christ is the goal, the aim, the intention, the real meaning and substance of the law --- apart from Him it cannot be properly understood at all."[28]

The other would say that "end" should be understood to mean "termination." Moo in support of this position writes:

> "The relationship between v. 4 and v. 3 shows that Paul wants to stress the discontinuity between Christ and the law. The Jews' striving for a righteousness of "their own,"

> based on the law (v.3), is wrong (among other reasons) because Christ has brought an end to the law and to the era of which it was the center. This is the same point that Paul has made in Romans 3:21: God's righteousness has been made manifest "apart from the law."[29]

Arnold Fruchtenbaum, in his book "Israelology," agrees with *telos* meaning "termination," He writes:

> "The Greek word for "end," *telos*, can mean either "termination" or "goal." Here, however, the evidence clearly favors the meaning of "end." For example, Thayer gives the primary meaning of *telos* as:
>
> > … *end*, i.e. a. *termination, the limit* at which a thing ceases to be, … in the Scriptures also of a temporal end; … Christ has brought the law to an end.
>
> Not only does Thayer give "termination" as the primary meaning of *telos*, he also includes Romans 10:4 as belonging to that category of usage. Nor is "goal" listed as a secondary or even tertiary in priority of usage; it is fourth on the list."[30]

Fruchtenbaum concludes his statement by saying:

> "In the final analysis, other Scriptures teach both truths: The Messiah is the goal of the law, but He is also the termination of the law. Since Christ is the end of the law, there is no justification through the law (Galatians 2:16). This, was always true of justification, but since the ending of the law, sanctification or perfection no longer comes through the law (Hebrews 7:19). Thus, it should be quite evident that the law ended in Christ. It cannot function in justification or sanctification. It has been rendered inoperative, especially for the believer."[31]

While I believe that Paul's main point in Romans 10:4 is that Christ is the termination of the law, it no longer has any validity regarding a believer being made right in God's sight -- justification, I think it is very important to note some points regarding Christ and the law as we conclude this section.

First, Christ being the "goal" of the law, while not the primary meaning in Romans 10:4, nevertheless is taught elsewhere in Scripture and must be understood in light of what the believing Israelite under the Mosaic Law comprehended. They knew that it was not doing the works of the law that made them right in God's sight, but rather God's gracious acceptance of the animal sacrifice as payment for their sins that brought them righteousness. That was what Paul is alluding to when he says in Gal 3:24-25:

> "Therefore the law was our tutor to bring us to Christ, that we might be justified by faith. But after faith has come, we are no longer under a tutor."

Every time an Israelite brought an animal sacrifice to the temple, he should have been reminded of the fact that it was God's provision for him, to enable him to have a righteousness that comes from faith. Those who understood that were part of the believing remnant.

Second, for the Jewish believer today, this is an important and controversial issue regarding what constitutes a Jewish expression of our faith. Are we to be "torah observant," and if so, what does that look like? Who or what makes that decision? If we begin from the point that the Torah is no longer binding on a person's life, that the Law of Moses has been rendered inoperative as a rule of life, that the Messiah is the end of the law, then the rule of liberty should be applied. Fruchtenbaum writes:

> "It is evident that the Jewish believer is free from the law and has a choice 'to keep or not to keep' in these areas. This approach allows for a variety of Messianic Jewish expressions and a variety of Jewish lifestyles rather than imposing one system upon all, and it avoids a potentially endless number of man-made laws. It is my hope that, rather than creating a new Mishnah, Jewish believers will study and teach the Law of the Messiah as found in the New Covenant, understanding and communicating it within its Jewish cultural and historical context. By allowing freedom and a variety of Jewish lifestyles, this will lead to equal acceptance of each other and unity in diversity. But if only one type of "Jewish lifestyle" is accepted as an

> absolute norm, it will cause divisions not only between Jewish and Gentile believers, but also between Jewish believers themselves. May God keep us from that."[32]

Jewish believers have the liberty to live as Jewish a lifestyle as they choose, however they choose to express it, and to live in light of their freedom in Messiah. Though the Messiah is indeed the "end of Torah," there is nothing unbiblical about Jewish believers expressing their Messianic faith as they choose, as long as it doesn't contradict Scripture. It is only when liberty and choice becomes obligation and compulsion that Scripture is abrogated.

CHAPTER 6

The Righteousness Of Faith

Continuing the thought of their zealousness for God but not according to knowledge, in this next sermon section Paul contrasts the righteousness that is based on doing the works of the law with the righteousness that is based on faith. He writes in Romans 10:5-7:

> "For Moses writes about the righteousness which is of the law, "The man who does those things shall live by them." But the righteousness of faith speaks in this way, "Do not say in your heart, 'Who will ascend into heaven?'" (that is, to bring Christ down from above) or, "'Who will descend into the abyss?'" (that is, to bring Christ up from the dead)."

Romans 10:5 begins with the word for, the Greek word *gár,* which Paul uses as the connection to the previous verse, so that what immediately follows is seen as explanation. When he says that "Moses writes about the righteousness which is of the law," he follows with a quote from the third book of the Penteteuch, Leviticus 18:5:

> "You shall therefore keep My statutes and My judgments, which if a man does, he shall live by them: I am the LORD."

Moo, discussing Paul's use of this quote writes:

> "His purpose in quoting Lev 18:5 is succinctly to summarize what for him is the essence of the law: blessing is contingent on obedience. It is the one who does the works required by the law who must find life through them. The emphasis lies on the word "doing" and not on the promise of "life." Paul states this principle as a warning. The Jew who refuses to submit to the righteousness of God in Christ, ignoring the fact that the law has come to its culmination in Christ and seeking to establish a relationship with God through the Law, must be content in seeking that relationship through "doing." Yet human doing, imperfect as even the most sincere

striving must be, is inadequate to bring a person into relationship with God --- as Paul has already shown in Romans 1:18-3:20."[33]

The person believing that they are able to earn salvation, the righteousness necessary to gain their way into heaven, must understand that the Bible teaches that there is absolutely no room for error. In order to attain to the righteousness of the law, a person must keep all the law, all the time, as James 2:10 confirms:

"For whoever shall keep the whole law, and yet stumble in one point, he is guilty of all."

Again quoting Moses, Paul now contrasts the righteousness of the law with the righteousness of faith, in Rom 10:6-8:

"But the righteousness of faith speaks in this way, "Do not say in your heart, 'Who will ascend into heaven?'" (that is, to bring Christ down from above) or, "'Who will descend into the abyss?'" (that is, to bring Christ up from the dead). But what does it say? "The word is near you, in your mouth and in your heart" (that is, the word of faith which we preach):"

The quote is from Deuteronomy 9:4 and Deuteronomy 30:11-14. With the quote from Deuteronomy 9:4, Paul wants his readers to connect these words with the context from which they come. In the verse, Moses warned the children of Israel that when they have taken possession of the land God was bringing them to, they must not think that somehow they earned it because of their own righteousness. With this first quote, Paul is implying a biblical support for his criticism of his "brethren according to the flesh," and their pursuit of a righteousness of the law.

Paul's use of the quotation of Deut 30:12-14 was to make the comparison of the giving of the law to the giving of the Messiah. This portion in Deuteronomy was part of Moses' charge to the generation of Israel about to enter the promised land. Blessings were promised for faith and obedience, and cursings would result from rejection and disobedience. John Witmer, in the Bible Knowledge Commentary, writes:

"The point of Moses' exhortation (Deut. 30:11) is that the generation to whom he was speaking had the message (it was very near you and in your mouth, Deut. 30:14) and could respond by faith (in your heart, Deut. 30:14) and walk with God in obedience. Since the Israelites in Moses' day had the message, they did not need to ask that it be brought down from heaven or that someone "cross the sea to get it" (Deut. 30:13). Instead, the word (Moses' instructions) was "near" them (Deut. 30:14)."[34]

In effect, Paul was saying that the same truth applied to his generation, and by implication all believers who read Romans. Just as the law was brought down to the people by Moses, so also Christ, the Messiah, has been brought down to earth, has come in the flesh (John 1:14). Therefore there was no need for anyone to ask, "Who will ascend into heaven?'" (that is, to bring Christ down from above). Also, since Christ has already been resurrected, there was no need to ask, "'Who will descend into the abyss?'" (that is, to bring Christ up from the dead). Kreloff summarizes this when he writes:

"The meaning of these words of Moses can be summed up this way: The knowledge of God's will is now accessible to you. You are not required to do the impossible, such as ascend to heaven or go beyond the sea. God's will is not unreachable. You do not have to go searching for something you cannot possibly attain. Paul's point was that righteousness by faith does not require us to scale the heavens to bring Christ down. Nor does it require us to go into Hades to raise Him from the dead. Both are impossibilities! The message of salvation is not far away and beyond reach. It is so near to us that it is actually in our mouths and hearts."[35]

The key point that Paul is communicating to us in v. 8 is that the message of righteousness by faith in Paul's day was "near" his readers, and this was "the word" of faith he was proclaiming. The Greek word translated "word" is *reema* literally "the spoken word." Thus the gospel, "the word of faith," as it is proclaimed and preached around the world is available and accessible. Mills commenting on v.8 writes:

"We need not climb heights or cross oceans to hear God's Word. It has been brought to us, we see it, we hear it; but, we must believe it, and we must confess with our lips that which we believe in our hearts. It is faith. It requires implicit trust and surrender of self. Faith is God's principle for attaining righteousness."[36]

In Romans 10:9-10, Paul explains the nearness of the "word of faith" by emphasizing the simplicity of the required response:

> "that if you confess with your mouth the Lord Jesus and believe in your heart that God has raised Him from the dead, you will be saved. For with the heart one believes unto righteousness, and with the mouth confession is made unto salvation."

Confessing with the mouth that Jesus is Lord is mentioned first, to be consistent with the order of the quotation from Deuteronomy 30:14 in Romans 10:8. The confession is an acknowledgement that God has come to earth as the man Jesus, and that Jesus Christ truly is God. The Greek word, *kurios*, translated Lord, in this context speaks of His deity. The NIV captures the idea of acknowledging Jesus is God in Romans 10:9, with the statement: "That if you confess with your mouth, "Jesus is Lord," The Greek word *homologeoo,* translated "confess," means more than just an initial walk down the aisle of a church to acknowledge Jesus as Savior. The implication for this confession with your mouth is that it is part of one's life to be confessing Jesus is Lord, part of one's daily witness, done at all times, under all circumstances, not being concerned for personal cost, testifying as to who He is.

Also essential is a true belief in one's heart that God raised Him from the dead. Notice the connection to Rom 10:6-7. 'Who will ascend into heaven?'" (that is, to bring Christ down). Confess with your mouth Jesus is Lord. 'Who will descend into the deep?'" (that is, to bring Christ up from the dead). Believe in your heart that God raised him from the dead. The result of this confession and belief is "you will be saved."

The true order of this process for salvation is given in verse 10:

> "For with the heart one believes unto righteousness, and with the mouth confession is made unto salvation."

Again the NIV is clearer in capturing the process for getting saved:

> "For it is with your heart that you believe and are justified, and it is with your mouth that you confess and are saved."

Salvation comes through acknowledging to God that Christ is God (Jesus is Lord), and believing in Him (God raised Him from the dead). Verse 10 is a transition as Paul now moves to making universal application of this general principal of salvation in Romans 10:11-13:

> "For the Scripture says, "Whoever believes on Him will not be put to shame." For there is no distinction between Jew and Greek, for the same Lord over all is rich to all who call upon Him. For "whoever calls on the name of the LORD shall be saved."

Quoting again from Isaiah 28:16, Paul makes a change from the original text and adds the Greek word *pás ho,* translated "whoever" or "everyone," in order to state the biblical truth that the gospel is a universal call. In Romans 3:23 Paul teaches that all are lost in sin and unable to attain to God's standard of perfection. Now here in Romans 10:11, Paul teaches that God makes salvation available in Christ for anyone who believes. The Greek phrase *ou kataischuntheésetai*, translated "will not be put to shame," refers to deliverance at the time of judgment. Those who put their faith and trust in Christ will have their trust in God prove to be well-founded and justified.

In Romans 10:12-13 Paul is more specific in describing the universality inherent in the gospel. He writes,

> "For there is no distinction between Jew and Greek, for the same Lord over all is rich to all who call upon Him. For "whoever calls on the name of the LORD shall be saved."

There is no distinction between Jew and Greek in sin and judgment as Paul has already taught in Romans 3:23, so there is also no distinction between them as far as who their Lord is and the grace that He offers them. The word Lord, *Kurios,* refers to Christ, to the Messiah. Clearly, Paul is teaching us that the Jewish person is just as lost as the Gentile person and just as desperately needs the Lord Jesus their Messiah. This same Lord and Messiah, who is over both Jew and Gentile, Paul says is "rich to all who call upon Him." Moo writes:

> "Paul frequently uses the language of "wealth" to connote the unlimited resources of God that He makes available to His people in and through His Son. Often, these riches are defined in terms of God's grace or mercy, and this is certainly Paul's intention here as well."[37]

The idea of calling on Him, from the Greek phrase *epikalouménous autón,* was used in secular Greek for asking someone for assistance, especially asking the gods for help or intervention. In this context, the assistance being asked of God, by both Jew and Gentile, is for His salvation.

Paul concludes this section with a quote from Joel 2:32: For "whoever calls on the name of the LORD shall be saved." The setting of the verse in Joel and its context has to do with the second coming of Jesus and the establishment of His Messianic Kingdom. Paul uses the truth of this verse even in its context to teach his key point. The one who calls upon the Lord, the one who seeks what God and God alone can give, that is the one who will be saved, and saved eternally. The actual verse in Joel seems to be talking about the remnant of Israel:

> "And it shall come to pass that whoever calls on the name of the LORD shall be saved. For in Mount Zion and in Jerusalem there shall be deliverance, as the LORD has said, Among the remnant whom the LORD calls."

But in Romans 10:13, Paul makes application to all people, Jew and Gentile, Israel and the Nations, when he says, "whoever calls on the name of the LORD shall be saved."

CHAPTER 7

How Beautiful Are The Feet Of Those Who Preach Good News!

Concluding Chapter 10, in this next sermon section Paul now goes back to discussing the plight of Israel. He writes in Rom 10:14-15:

> "How then shall they call on Him in whom they have not believed? And how shall they believe in Him of whom they have not heard? And how shall they hear without a preacher? And how shall they preach unless they are sent? As it is written: "How beautiful are the feet of those who preach the gospel of peace, Who bring glad tidings of good things!"

Moo, describing this portion writes:

> "Verse 14 and the first part of v. 15 contain a series of four parallel rhetorical questions, each beginning with the interrogative "how." By repeating the verb from the end of one question at the beginning of the next, Paul creates a connected chain of steps that must be followed if a person is to be saved. Paul, in v. 13 has asserted a universally applicable principle: that salvation is granted to all who call on the Lord. But people cannot call on the Lord if they do not believe in him, and they cannot believe in him if they do not hear the word that proclaims Christ."[38]

This portion is usually preached as a good general missions sermon. If people are to be saved, a preacher must be sent, the message must be preached, the message must be heard, and the message must be believed. But let's not lose sight of what Paul has been speaking about since Romans 9. This portion is about Paul sharing his heart regarding the lostness of his kindred, "his brethren according to the flesh." It's as though Paul is trying to convince these Roman believers to share the gospel with his brethren, the people of Israel. Why would he have to do that? Because of the opposition from the Jewish people and anti-semitic feelings which were beginning to fester and creep into the early church.

This is an important series of questions that Paul raises regarding the lost state of Israel and the Jewish people. How are the Jewish people going to call on the Lord Jesus Christ as their Messiah when they have not heard of or believed in Him? Sanford Mills writes:

> "All they have known of Christ and the hordes of His false followers through the ages and until now, has been persecution and proscription, torture and torment, bloodshed and butchery. Throughout the centuries Israel has been hearing of Christ in mockery, primarily from the lips of their persecutors. They have called Jews Christ-killers." The Jewish person has repeatedly asked the question, How can Jesus be the Messiah of Israel when His followers hate us and persecute us?"[39]

The one truth about Jesus that I was sure of, growing up as a young Jewish boy in Brooklyn, New York, was that He was not for me. I simply did not believe that He was for anyone but the Gentiles. The Gentile people I knew, who I believed were all Christians, didn't say or do anything to convince me otherwise.. They all seemed to consider us Christ-killers, some expressing this more vocally than others, and they all seemed to impart the message that Jesus belonged to them. This was especially true during Good Friday. No one, until I was twenty-eight years old, ever told me that Jesus was the Jewish Messiah. No one ever told me that He was the long awaited one.

That brings us to Paul's next question, "And how shall they believe in Him of whom they have not heard?" Israel as a nation, the majority of Jewish people individually, have not heard the true message of the Gospel. In Paul's time, though, that was less true than it is today; because Jesus' life, death, and resurrection were not only events that were still talked about, they were events that were still fresh in people's minds. He was still considered Jewish and His followers were as well.

Today, on the contrary, the majority of Jewish people have not heard a clear presentation of the gospel message or believe Jesus is Jewish. They don't own or read a New Testament and they rarely read the Old Testament. They stay away from churches, they don't watch Christian television, and they don't listen to Christian radio. They have not heard of Jesus as their Jewish Messiah.

In order for Israel to be saved they need to call upon the Lord. In order for them to call upon the Lord they need to believe. In order for them to believe they need to hear the gospel of Jesus the Messiah preached to them, which brings us to the third question of Paul's, in Romans 10:14, "And how shall they hear without a preacher? There needs to be a concerted effort to preach to and evangelize the Jewish people. That's what Paul is inferring in Romans 1:16, when he speaks of the priority of Jewish evangelism:

> "For I am not ashamed of the gospel of Christ, for it is the power of God to salvation for everyone who believes, for the Jew first and also for the Greek."

The gospel being to or for the Jew first means that the Jew especially needs to hear the message of Jesus the Jewish Messiah. Who more than they need to know that their Messiah has come to die for all our sins, and He's coming again to reign on the throne of David in Jerusalem for one thousand years. It is an especially Jewish message and Jews, as the Holy Spirit works in their hearts, will respond to it. Which brings us to Paul's fourth and last rhetorical question in Romans 10:15, "And how shall they preach unless they are sent?"

There needs to be a concerted effort on the part of the church to reach the Jewish people for the gospel of Jesus. In order to do that, preachers need to be sent. Churches and mission organizations are sending people to the four corners of the world to reach the heathen, the unreached people groups, and that's a good thing. But the church, as a whole, has been lax in making an effort to preach the gospel to the people through whom Jesus came. There is very little being done to reach the Jewish people. Listen again to Paul's words in Romans 10:14-15:

> "How then shall they call on Him in whom they have not believed? And how shall they believe in Him of whom they have not heard? And how shall they hear without a preacher? And how shall they preach unless they are sent? As it is written: "How beautiful are the

feet of those who preach the gospel of peace, who bring glad tidings of good things!"

The Old Testament passage quoted by Paul at the end of Romans 10:15 is from Isaiah 52:7:

"How beautiful upon the mountains are the feet of him who brings good news, who proclaims peace, who brings glad tidings of good things, who proclaims salvation, who says to Zion, "Your God reigns!"

This Isaiah passage is often used again to generically speak of the importance of evangelism to all people. But clearly one must make primary application to Israel, as Paul suggests here. Mills commenting on this Isaiah quotation writes:

"Isaiah 52:1-10 looks forward to the establishment of the Davidic kingdom which is the everlasting kingdom of Messiah. Even Jewish Rabbis have taught that this passage is messianic, a prophecy to be fulfilled at the time when King Messiah will come. Not only will Israel rejoice, but the Gentile nations will also rejoice at the completed revelation of the salvation of the Lord in the person of Jesus the Messiah. What joy! What gladness this will bring! In v.15 Paul makes application of the world-wide nature of the Isaiah passage to its personal and immediate relevancy. Just as the world will rejoice in the Millennial Kingdom over Jehovah's salvation, so does the individual Jew and Gentile in this present time rejoice in their personal salvation."[40]

Warren Wiersbe also commenting on the application to Israel of this quotation from Isaiah writes:

"Isaiah used this statement for a *future* event—the return of Christ and the establishing of His glorious kingdom. "Thy God reigneth!" (Read Isa. 52:7-10.) The messenger with the beautiful feet announced that God had defeated Israel's enemies and that Messiah was reigning from Jerusalem. But Paul used the quotation in a *present* application: the messengers of the Gospel taking the Good News to Israel today. The "peace" spoken of is "peace with God" (Rom. 5:1) and the peace Christ has effected between Jews and Gentiles by forming the one body, the church (Eph. 2:13-17). The remedy for Israel's

rejection is in hearing the Word of the Gospel and
believing on Jesus Christ."[41]

Preachers must be sent to all people, but we must not forget the priority of necessity of Romans 1:16, that the gospel is to the Jew first, and they especially need the message of the Messiah. Jewish people won't hear the gospel message unless it's preached to them. Jewish people won't believe in Jesus as their Messiah unless they hear the message. Jewish people won't call on the Lord unless they believe. And Jewish people won't be saved unless they call on the Lord. Paul understood what was at stake and he was heartbroken over it.

In Romans 10:16 Paul deals with additional thoughts on Israel's unbelief. In essence, he's explained the various stages of evangelism. The preacher is sent, the gospel is preached, the message is heard, the message is believed, the person calls on the name of the Lord and is saved. Now he answers the question, "How then is Israel's unbelief to be explained?" He writes in Romans 10:16-17:

"But they have not all obeyed the gospel. For Isaiah
says, "LORD, who has believed our report?" So then
faith comes by hearing, and hearing by the word of God."

In verse 16 Paul is reiterating the notion of the remnant. Notice he doesn't say, "all Israel did not hearken." By saying, "they have not all obeyed the gospel," he's implying that some did. In fact, a study of the Book of Acts reveals that a great multitude of Israelites believed in Jesus as their Messiah. At the end of Peter's Pentecost sermon, three thousand Israelites believed. Luke's account of this event, beginning with Peter's conclusion, is in Acts 2:36-41:

"Therefore let all the house of Israel know assuredly
that God has made this Jesus, whom you crucified,
both Lord and Christ." Now when they heard this,
they were cut to the heart, and said to Peter and the
rest of the apostles, "Men and brethren, what shall
we do?" Then Peter said to them,"Repent, and let
every one of you be baptized in the name of Jesus
Christ for the remission of sins; and you shall receive
the gift of the Holy Spirit. For the promise is to you
and to your children, and to all who are afar off, as

> many as the Lord our God will call." And with many other words he testified and exhorted them, saying, "Be saved from this perverse generation." Then those who gladly received his word were baptized; and that day about three thousand souls were added to them."

In Acts 4, 5, and 6, the majority of people we see coming to faith in Christ, numbering in the thousands, were Israelites. In fact, first century historian Josephus states that more than one-third of the Jewish population of the world at the end of the first century were followers of Jesus. So clearly, "they have not all obeyed the gospel," but a large and substantial remnant did. Paul then quotes Isaiah 53:1, to show that Israel's unbelief was foretold centuries earlier by the prophet.

Paul, in verse 17, summarizes the importance of bringing the Gospel message to the Jew first and also to the Gentile. But he does it by emphasizing the importance of hearing and believing. "So then faith comes by hearing, and hearing by the word of God." Commenting on this verse, Cranfield writes:

> "The quotation speaks of believing a message. But a message's being believed involves an intermediate occurrence between the message's being uttered and its being believed, namely, its being heard. So in v. 17 Paul draws out *(ára)* what is implied in his quotation, applying it to the matter in hand. Faith results from hearing the message, and the hearing of the message comes about through the Word of Christ (i.e., through Christ's speaking the message by the mouths of His messengers). This corroborates what was said in vvs. 14-15, but it is not a mere pointless repetition, since in it hearing becomes the hinge, so that it leads naturally into v. 18."[42]

The challenge given by Paul to the Romans, and by implication to every believer, is for us to see the importance of proclaiming the message of salvation through Jesus Christ, the Messiah of Israel and Savior of the World. As valuable as it is to get Bibles into the hands of various people groups, the priority ought to be to send preachers and evangelists to proclaim the Gospel message to the uttermost parts of the earth. That's true for world evangelization and it's certainly true for Jewish evangelism. The preacher needs to be sent, the Gospel message needs to be proclaimed, the message needs to be heard, the message needs to be believed, and the hearer needs to call on the Lord to be saved. "So then faith comes by hearing, and hearing by the word of God." (Romans 10:17)

Developing his thoughts on why Israel has not believed, Paul submits and then rejects two possible explanations. He then offers his own explanation as he sets the stage for Chapter 11. He writes in Romans 10:18-21:

> "But I say, have they not heard? Yes indeed: "Their sound has gone out to all the earth, And their words to the ends of the world." But I say, did Israel not know? First Moses says: "I will provoke you to jealousy by those who are not a nation, I will move you to anger by a foolish nation." But Isaiah is very bold and says: "I was found by those who did not seek Me; I was made manifest to those who did not ask for Me." But to Israel he says: "All day long I have stretched out My hands to a disobedient and contrary people."

In these verses, again Paul is answering anticipated questions, objections which might possibly be raised. First, in Rom 10:18, the question of whether or not Israel has heard, since as Paul has stated in v. 17, "faith comes by hearing:"

> "But I say, have they not heard? Yes indeed: "Their sound has gone out to all the earth, And their words to the ends of the world."

The verse quoted in Romans 10:18 is Psalm 19:4. In using this Psalm, which in its first part speaks of God's revelation to the world in the heavens and in nature, Paul is not necessarily using it in its original context, but rather applying it in a general way to the proclaiming of the gospel message. Moo writes:

> "His application probably rests on a general analogy: as God's word of general revelation has been proclaimed over all the earth, so God's word of special revelation, in the gospel, has been spread over all the earth. His intention is not to interpret the verse of the Psalm, but to use its language, with the "echoes" of God's revelation that it awakes, to assert the universal preaching of the gospel."[43]

So, what does Paul mean when he says in Rom 10:18, "Their sound has gone out to all the earth, and their words to the ends of the world." Paul certainly doesn't mean that the "Great Commission" has been fulfilled and the gospel has been proclaimed to all the nations. Why then would he say, later in Romans 15, that his plan was to take a missionary journey to Spain. The answer, I believe, is that he was speaking in hyperbole.

Paul uses similar phrasing in Col 1:23:

> "if indeed you continue in the faith, grounded and steadfast, and are not moved away from the hope of the gospel which you heard, which was preached to every creature under heaven, of which I, Paul, became a minister."

Paul obviously doesn't believe that every living creature has heard the gospel, but rather, as far as he was aware, the gospel had been proclaimed everywhere in the known world. So in regards to Israel, Paul's contention was that as far as he was concerned, the gospel was proclaimed wherever there were Jewish people. Stott writes:

> "Since Paul is here alluding to the spread of the good news in Jewry, however, it may be better to understand Paul's claim as what F.F. Bruce has called 'representative universalism', meaning that 'wherever there were Jews', and in particular wherever a Jewish community existed, there the gospel had been preached. So the Jews have heard; they cannot blame their not believing on their not hearing."[44]

While the first question that Paul was addressing had to do with whether or not Israel heard the gospel, the second question, addressed in Rom 10:19, had to do with whether or not Israel understood the message.

> "But I say, did Israel not know? First Moses says: "I will provoke you to jealousy by those who are not a nation, I will move you to anger by a foolish nation."

The question at the beginning of the verse, "did Israel not know," is translated in the NIV, "did Israel not understand." The Greek word, *égno,* from Thayer's Greek Lexicon means "to know, understand, perceive, have knowledge of." Another way of asking the question is, Was Israel's hearing simply a superficial hearing, one that did not bring understanding, knowledge, and perception of the gospel? Isn't that what Paul alludes to later on in Romans 11, when he quotes from Isaiah 6:9-10?

> "And He said, "Go, and tell this people: 'Keep on hearing, but do not understand; Keep on seeing, but do not perceive.' "Make the heart of this people dull, And their ears heavy, And shut their eyes; Lest they see with their eyes, And hear with their ears, And understand with their heart, And return and be healed."

Rather than speaking about a superficial understanding, the Isaiah quote is speaking of those of Israel whose hearts were hardened, who, like Pharaoh, were rebellious and disobedient to God. God allowed their hearts to be hardened so that they simply would not believe His message of salvation. It would be the remnant who would hear and believe and be saved.

So, what then is Paul saying with Romans 10:19? To understand that, we need to examine the Old Testament quote that he's using. The passage is found in Deuteronomy 32:21 and in its entirety it reads:

> "They have provoked Me to jealousy by what is not God; They have moved Me to anger by their foolish idols. But I will provoke them to jealousy by those who are not a nation; I will move them to anger by a foolish nation."

Though repeatedly warned by Moses of God's promises of curses for disobedience, Israel continued throughout her Old Testament history to live as though she never knew or believed. She acted as though she was a people who didn't know God. God's promise is that He would use a non-nation, a people of no understanding, a foolish people, to make Israel angry and provoke them to jealousy. The passage is reminiscent of an earlier quotation of Hosea in Romans 9:25-26 when Paul wrote:

> "I will call them My people, who were not My people, And her beloved, who was not beloved." "And it shall come to pass in the place where it was said to them, ' You are not My people,' There they shall be called sons of the living God."

Though Israel always knew what was expected of her as a nation and a people, through the Mosaic Law, though she clearly understood, she was never able to sustain it and put it into practice. Because Israel became such a disobedient nation, the Gentiles therefore would have the opportunity to hear and respond to the gospel message of the Messiah of Israel. That is what Paul is affirming as he quotes now from Isaiah in Romans 10:20:

> "But Isaiah is very bold and says: "I was found by those who did not seek Me; I was made manifest to those who did not ask for Me."

This is from Isaiah 65:1 and reads in its entirety as follows:

> "I was sought by those who did not ask for Me; I was found by those who did not seek Me. I said, 'Here I am, here I am,' To a nation that was not called by My name."

With the added portion of Isaiah 65:1, we see God reversing the roles between Himself and the Gentiles. It is not they who are asking, and seeking, and knocking, but rather God. It is He who says, "Here I am. What an incredible picture of grace. God is taking the initiative in making Himself known to a people who have absolutely no desire or care to know Him. Mills writes:

> "While the Gentiles were in this depraved condition, God manifested Himself to them. He called the Apostle Paul to go and preach the Gospel to the Gentiles, and then commanded Peter to visit a Gentile's house and preach to him and his family. Peter was shocked and amazed to think that God would bestow His mercy upon a depraved Gentile, one who was of a people who were no people."[45]

Paul shows that Israel's rejection of the gospel was not because they didn't hear. Israel's rejection of the gospel was not because they didn't understand. Rather, Israel's rejection of the gospel was because of stubborn and willful disobedience. Paul now concludes this chapter, which has detailed Israel's unbelief, with God's response to Israel's rejection of Him, found in Rom 10:21:

> "But to Israel he says: "All day long I have stretched out My hands to a disobedient and contrary people."

This is a continuation of the Isaiah quote, with the beginning of Isaiah 65:2. Here we see God not just allowing Himself to be found, as with the Gentiles, but rather He is vigorously and dynamically holding out his hands to them. Like the father of the prodigal son, God is waiting with open arms for His wayward child to return to Him. But the response of the majority is not apathy, as with the Gentiles who didn't seek Him or ask for Him, the response is negative, resistant, defiant, and dismissive. Stott writes:

"They are determined to remain a disobedient and obstinate people. We feel God's dismay, his grief."[46]

The picture we have as Chapter 10 closes is one of a grieving God over the lostness of a people who, except for a small remnant, refuse to return to Him. They choose to remain as they are, a disobedient and contrary people. Though their promised Messiah has come, they choose to reject Him and not believe their Scriptures. In chapter nine, Paul ascribed the unbelief of the people of Israel to God's election, because of which many were passed by and only a remnant believed. Now in chapter ten, Paul attributes Israel's unbelief to their own willful disobedience. They heard the message, they understood the message, they chose to reject it and would not believe. The paradox of divine sovereignty, (Eph 1:4) and human responsibility, (John 3:16) remains

For those of us in full-time Jewish ministry this picture of the rejection of their Messiah by the Jewish people is all too familiar. Though we grieve over their lostness, though we feel rejected as we continually bring the good news to our Jewish brethren, though the message that we proclaim, for the most part, falls on deaf ears, though our motives are often misunderstood and misrepresented, it would be good for us to meditate on the picture that Paul leaves with us at the end of the chapter. The picture is of a grieving God continually opening His arms and His heart to a people who simply choose to say no. No one is more broken hearted over the lost state of Israel than God Himself. Mills concludes his commentary on chapter ten by writing:

"Does this mean that God made a mistake when He led His Chosen People out of Egyptian slavery and into the Promised Land of Canaan? Have God's plans, program and purposes for Israel gone amiss? Have God's covenants and promises to the patriarchs and Israel been negated through Israel's sinful actions? Has God been caught unaware? Is God's program now nullified because of Israel's refusal to hearken to His Word? All this is contained in the quotation of Isaiah 65:2, and in Romans 10:21. And all of the questions which may have been in Paul's mind are answered in Chapter Eleven."[47]

CHAPTER 8

Has God Cast Away His People?

With the beginning of Chapter 11, the next sermon section commences with Paul continuing the discussion he began in the closing portion of Chapter 10. The picture that he left us with, is that of a grieving God continually opening His arms and His heart to a people who simply choose to say no to Him. In light of Israel, as a nation, rejecting their God and Messiah, Paul begins by writing in Romans 11:1:

> "I say then, has God cast away His people? Certainly not! For I also am an Israelite, of the seed of Abraham, of the tribe of Benjamin."

One might suppose, based on the fact that the majority of Israel has rejected God, that He had rejected them. Certainly with the fact that the gospel was finding more fertile soil among the Gentiles than the Jews in Paul's time, and even by application to our own day, the evidence would seem to point in that direction. But this will be emphatically proven by Paul to be false. Israel's rejection is only partial and the believing remnant remains.

Today the question might be asked, because of Israel's rejection of Jesus their Messiah, are the promises originally given to the patriarchs now negated. Is God finished with the Jewish people? Are God's promises given to a disobedient Israel now transferred to the church, the new Israel? Mills comments on this question regarding Israel's rejection of God when he writes:

> "Does this mean that the promises of God made to the Patriarchs and to Israel must be altered, that is to say, spiritualized, to suit this age? Must the names Zion, Jerusalem, Canaan, now be made to mean Heaven? The Apostle's answer rings from the rooftops of eternity, No! God Forbid! Impossible! The Old Testament is not nullified, and God is not through with the Jews."[48]

As I've said previously, Paul's response in the Greek, *meé génoito,* is the strongest possible negative, translated in different versions of the Bible as, "certainly not," "God forbid," "by no means," "not at all," "may it never be." The very thought of anyone believing that God could or would reject the Jewish people was virtually blasphemous to Paul. The implication of that possibility to Paul is unthinkable. But what does Paul offer as proof to point out how ridiculous and repugnant that question is? He points to his own salvation in Romans 11:1:

> "For I also am an Israelite, of the seed of Abraham, of the tribe of Benjamin."

Paul makes it perfectly clear here that he is identifying himself with Israel. He is a descendant of Abraham, from the only tribe that stayed faithful to Judah, the tribe of Benjamin. Paul himself, as a Jewish believer in Jesus the Messiah, along with every other Jewish believer in Jesus who has ever lived, is living proof that God is not finished with the Jewish people. God is not finished with the Jewish people, Jewish people can and still do get saved, and all you have to do is look at me as proof, Paul is saying. Paul is telling us in as strong a way as he knows how that Jewish people are savable. In fact, we can take this argument one step further. If Paul, the one who was persecuting the early believers as the Pharisee Saul, can get saved, certainly, it is clear that any Jewish person can get saved.

It is important to stop for a moment and take stock of what Paul is saying here in Romans 11:1. There is no way that Jewish people are unable to get saved. Paul is proof of that, the three thousand at Pentecost who got saved are proof of that, and every Jewish believer in Jesus today is proof of that. So then, if Paul's argument here is that Jewish people can and still do get saved, then Paul is clearly telling us that apart from Christ, apart from the Messiah, Jewish people, like everyone else, are desperately lost. Certainly, Romans 10:1 is proof that Paul believed that Jewish people were lost without Messiah when he states:

> "Brethren, my heart's desire and prayer to God for Israel is that they may be saved."

Without question, this was the reason why Paul, as stated in Romans 9:2, had "great sorrow and unceasing grief in his heart." Paul understood that everyone needs Jesus, and the Jewish people are no exception. Therefore, anyone arguing that

Jewish people don't need Jesus, that they are right with God apart from the Messiah, are arguing against the clear teaching of the Apostle Paul and of the Scripture. They are arguing heresy and perpetrating the worse form of anti-semitism imaginable. Nothing can be more hateful than withholding the gospel of the Jewish Messiah from the Jewish people.

As Paul continues his teaching in Romans 11:2, he is in essence, answering his own rhetorical question in v. 1, as he writes, "God has not cast away His people whom He foreknew." To grasp what Paul is teaching here, there must be an understanding of what he means when he makes the statement, "His people whom He foreknew." The Greek word *proégnoo,* translated foreknew, suggests a predetermined and preplanned choosing and setting apart in love, as shown in Amos 3:2. "You only have I known of all the families of the earth. Moo, commenting on the meaning of foreknew writes:

> "The temporal prefix 'fore' (pro-) indicates further that God's choosing of Israel took place before any action or status on the part of Israel that might have qualified her for God's choice. How could God reject a people whom he in a gracious act of choice had made his own?"[49]

Who then are the recipients of this gracious choice of God's? How should the clause be understood? If it is to be understood in a restrictive sense as Calvin understood it, then the recipients would be those members of the people of Israel who are the objects of God's election. Cranfield comments on this and answers the question as to who are the recipients of this gracious choice of God's when he writes,

> "In spite of the fact that vv. 4-7 do go on to differentiate between an elect remnant and the rest of the people, this interpretation is most unlikely; for it is hardly to be disputed that v. 1 refers to Israel as a whole, and it is unnatural to give it a different sense in v. 2. We take it then that the relative clause refers to the general election of the people as a whole, and indicates a further ground for denying that God has cast off His people. The fact that God foreknew them (i.e., deliberately joined them to Himself in faithful love) excludes the possibility of His casting them off."[50]

As Paul continues his reasoning on why God is not finished with Israel, at the end of Romans 11:2 through v. 4, he again makes reference to the subject of the remnant:

> "Or do you not know what the Scripture says of Elijah, how he pleads with God against Israel, saying, "LORD, they have killed Your prophets and torn down Your altars, and I alone am left, and they seek my life"? But what does the divine response say to him? "I have reserved for Myself seven thousand men who have not bowed the knee to Baal."

Using the phrase, "or do you not know," implies that Paul believes that his readers are going to be familiar with the Scripture to which he will refer to, and its application to his argument. The portion Paul is using as illustration is the story of King Ahab's attack on the prophets of the Lord and his wife Jezebel's threats against Elijah. Following the slaughter of the prophets by Ahab, Jezebel threatens Elijah with the same fate that befell those prophets in 1 Kings 19:1-2:

> "And Ahab told Jezebel all that Elijah had done, also how he had executed all the prophets with the sword. Then Jezebel sent a messenger to Elijah, saying, "So let the gods do to me, and more also, if I do not make your life as the life of one of them by tomorrow about this time."

After fleeing to the wilderness to escape Jezebel, Elijah is ministered to by an angel of God, and then when Elijah is asked by the Lord why he was hiding in a cave, he responds by lamenting his terrible plight to the Lord. Paul quotes 1 Kings 19:10 in Romans 11:3:

> So he said, "I have been very zealous for the LORD God of hosts; for the children of Israel have forsaken Your covenant, torn down Your altars, and killed Your prophets with the sword. I alone am left; and they seek to take my life."

How does Paul use this Old Testament portion to make application to what he's teaching regarding Israel? The parallels are very interesting. In the Old Testament portion, Israel has reached its spiritual low point under its most evil king Ahab, and his even more evil wife, Jezebel. Elijah is emotionally drained and feeling as though the situation for Israel is hopeless. In the same way, one might say to Paul, the Israel of his day was in a hopeless state. But look again at Paul's next quotation, in Romans 11:4:

> But what does the divine response say to him? "I have reserved for Myself seven thousand men who have not bowed the knee to Baal."

This is an abridged version of 1 Kings 19:18, where God says:

> "Yet I have reserved seven thousand in Israel, all whose knees have not bowed to Baal, and every mouth that has not kissed him."

Though Elijah thought that perhaps he was the only one of his people left that was truly following after God, God showed him that wasn't true. There was a small remnant, only seven thousand, but nevertheless, a group of people who had not fallen prey to the spiritual deprivation of Ahab and Jezebel. Just as God would respond to Elijah about a remnant bringing hope to Israel, in the same way, Paul will show that it is through the remnant that there is hope for Israel. Moo writes:

> "It is possible that Paul also finds a parallel between Elijah and himself: each is a key salvation-historical figure, is confronted with the apparent downfall of spiritual Israel, but finds new hope in God's preservation of a remnant of true believers. For God's preservation of a remnant is not only evidence of his present faithfulness to Israel; it is also a pledge of hope for the future of the people."[51]

In Romans 11:5-6, Paul makes application to his own situation from that of the Elijah portion which he's been talking about.

> "Even so then, at this present time there is a remnant according to the election of grace. And if by grace, then it is no longer of works; otherwise grace is no longer grace. But if it is of works, it is no longer grace; otherwise work is no longer work."

In essence, Romans 11:5 is saying, that in the same way that there were seven thousand who did not bow the knee to Baal in

Elijah's time, there is now a similar group from the nation of Israel, certainly in Paul's time larger than seven thousand, who are followers of the Messiah. And by implication, in the same way that there was a remnant of believers in Jesus as the Messiah in Paul's time, there is also a remnant of believers in our own time. God has always had a faithful remnant of followers from among Israel. Cranfield writes:

> "The existence of a remnant, whose faithfulness was their own meritorious achievement, would have had no particularly hopeful significance for the unfaithful majority. But, precisely because this remnant was preserved in accordance with the election of grace and not on the basis of works, its existence was a pledge of God's continuing interest in, and care for, the nation, a sign of God's faithfulness to His election of Israel as a whole."[52]

Paul's distinction between grace and works is very important and reiterates what he has already stated in Romans 9:31-32:

> "but Israel, pursuing the law of righteousness, has not attained to the law of righteousness. Why? Because they did not seek it by faith, but as it were, by the works of the law. For they stumbled at that stumbling stone."

The reason Israel had stumbled over Jesus the Messiah was because they did not understand their salvation was on the basis of grace through faith as Paul writes in Ephesians 2:8-9:

> "For by grace you have been saved through faith, and that not of yourselves; it is the gift of God, not of works, lest anyone should boast."

No matter how sincere a person may be in trying to get saved through the works of the Law, they will always fail, because no one, other than Jesus, has ever been able to keep the Law perfectly. The remnant are those who have come to understand the truth that grace and works must be mutually exclusive. Mills, commenting on the remnant, writes:

> "The first six verses of chapter 11 add up to the conclusion that God is not through with the Jews; that He has not cast them off as a nation; that there is a faithful remnant in Israel and that there always has been and will

> continue to be; and this remnant has been reserved by God in this age;"[53]

Paul concludes his discussion on the "remnant according to the election of grace." beginning in Romans 11:7:

> "What then? Israel has not obtained what it seeks; but the elect have obtained it, and the rest were blinded."

The Greek phrase, *Tí oún*, translated 'What then,' serves as a transition to what follows. With this question Paul is essentially asking, What conclusions can we make here? The statement, "Israel has not obtained what it seeks," again refers to what's been said in Romans 9:31:

> "Israel, pursuing the law of righteousness, has not attained to the law of righteousness. "

Israel, throughout biblical history, has been trying to become righteous in the sight of God through, as they see it, keeping the Mosaic Law. Many Jewish people today continue to try and become righteous in God's sight through the Law. In spite of the fact that they have done it, in many cases, with great zealousness, they have never reached their goal. What an ironic situation! Israel, as a people, have tried and continue to try and reach God through 'pursuing the law of righteousness,' through good works. Only the elect, "the remnant according to the election of grace," have obtained it. Because of God's sovereign choosing there was, and is, a saved remnant of Israel who are the ones that have obtained what the vast majority of Israel have not.

What has happened to the vast majority of Israel? Paul says in Romans 11:7, "the rest were blinded." What does that mean? The Greek word, *epooroótheesan,* translated "blinded," more literally means to grow hard or callous, and is translated in other versions as "hardened." The Amplified Bible says, "the rest of them became callously indifferent." The picture is of a callousness, a hardness toward the things of God, causing them to be unable to see or comprehend. Paul is declaring Israel to be in a state of spiritual insensitivity.

Since the verb, "to harden," is in the aorist indicative passive, it tells us that the hardening process was brought upon Israel by an outside agency, rather than Israel hardening herself. In this case, it's God who has hardened or blinded Israel. Just as God hardened Pharaoh's hard heart against Israel before Moses ever started on his journey, so also did He harden national Israel's proud and hard hearts against Himself. Stott writes:

> "There can be little doubt that Paul meant that they were hardened by God (since the next verse says that God gave them a spirit of stupor). Nevertheless, as with the hardening of Pharaoh and those he represented, a judicial process is in mind (a retribution, in fact, 11:9) by which God gives people up to their own stubbornness. What this 'hardening' means in practice Paul goes on to indicate from two Old Testament quotations, both of which refer to eyes which cannot see."[54]

The first of these quotes, taken from Deuteronomy 29:4 and Isaiah 29:10, is in Romans 11:8:

> "Just as it is written: "God has given them a spirit of stupor, Eyes that they should not see And ears that they should not hear, To this very day."

With the phrase, "Just as it is written," Paul is telling us that he will be illustrating the concept of the blindness or hardening of Israel with Scripture. The statement, "God has given them a spirit of stupor," is taken from Isaiah 29:10:

> "For the LORD has poured out on you the spirit of deep sleep, and has closed your eyes, namely, the prophets; And He has covered your heads, namely, the seers."

The Greek word translated stupor in Romans 11:8, *katanúxeoos,* emphasizes a dulling of the spiritual senses. Vincent's New Testament Word Studies says that in the context of this verse it means "a stupefaction following a wound or blow."[55] In other words, it is God who is causing this spirit of stupor or spiritual apathy to be upon Israel, as though they were receiving a sharp blow from Him. When one observes a Jewish person's complete apathy and indifference and, in many cases, hostility toward Jesus, the spirit of stupor becomes very evident. It is clearly seen at the time of Paul as well, as he describes what it looks like in Romans 11:8. Quoting from Deut 29:4, he writes:

> "Eyes that they should not see And ears that they should not hear, to this very day."

To the average Jewish person today, as it was in Paul's time, though they see and hear the Gospel message, they don't really perceive it. They erroneously believe that it is not for them. They look with their eyes, but they don't really see. And they listen with their ears, but they don't really hear. They are indifferent to the appeal and are blinded to its truth. That is what the spirit of stupor looks like. Mills moreover writes:

> "A careless reader of Scripture could, at this point, stumble into a false assumption that the 'hardening' process in Israel was the result of her own human frailty or the work of her self-willed leaders, whereas a careful study of the succeeding verses will show that the 'hardening'process was brought about wholly in accordance with God's plan and purpose, as operative today as it was in the past."[56]

God's motive for the 'hardening' will certainly become evident in verse 11, as well as His purpose for continuing to harden Israel today. If God willed it to be so, Israel today, as a people, could recover from her spiritual blindness and respond to God's revealed truth in the gospels. God has a purpose in not doing that now. In the meantime, it is the calling of the evangelical church as we will see in Romans 11:11 and following, to be effectively witnessing to the Jewish community and reaching the remnant.

The second of the quotes, taken from Psalm 69:22-23, is Romans 11:9-10:

> And David says: " Let their table become a snare and a trap, A stumbling block and a recompense to them. Let their eyes be darkened, so that they do not see, And bow down their back always."

Psalm 69 is quoted often in the New Testament and is considered one of the most important of the Messianic Psalms. Similar to Psalm 22, it is a lament of the Messiah's suffering, His anguish and grief. There also is an imprecatory aspect to it, as David asks God to curse his enemies who would cause that suffering. Paul's use of it here suggests that those of Israel who have not responded to the gospel have had the tables turned on them. Rather than being the persecuted for God, because of her rejection of the Messiah she has become the persecutor of God. The imagery of the table becoming a snare and a trap has to do with that which was the very source of their blessing is now the opposite to them. MacArthur writes:

> "The Jews considered God's Word, in particular the Torah, to be their spiritual sustenance --- which indeed it was. But because of their rebellious unbelief, that Word became a judgment on them, a stumbling block and a retribution."[57]

The second aspect of the imprecation has to do with God's hardening or blinding of Israel. Just as David, in Psalm 69, had prayed, in righteous indignation over the sins of his own people, Paul again alludes to the blindness or hardening of Israel by God. Because Israel refused to see the truth of God's Word in Messiah Jesus, God hardened or blinded Israel, allowing her own rebellion to come to fruition. The result of this blindness is having their backs bowed down or bent forever.

There are various interpretations of what the back is bent from. Some say it's from the burden of sin or guilt over the rejection of the Messiah. Some say it's from cowering with fear. Others say it is a picture of the blind man bent over, groping to find his way in the darkness. The last interpretation seems to fit the illustration best. Whatever the interpretation, Paul is going to clearly teach that this hardening or blindness is only in part, and will only be temporary. There will come a time when Israel, the Jewish people, will truly recognize Jesus as her Messiah. Mills concludes this portion by writing:

> "God's eternal purpose is the motivating factor in the blinding and hardening of Israel. Because of God's great love for Israel, upon which His purposes for her salvation are based, the Gentiles are made to be the recipients of God's love, mercy, and grace, as we shall see. This truth is developed further along in this chapter. What we need to remember is that we are not to despair or neglect our witness because of this "hardening process" which is still Israel's lot under God. Let us rather rejoice that there is still "a remnant according to the election of grace," and preach the gospel to Jews and Gentiles alike."[58]

CHAPTER 9

The Gentile Great Commission

Continuing with the next sermon section Paul will deal with the important question of the purpose of Gentile salvation and begins by writing in Romans 11:11:

> "I say then, have they stumbled that they should fall? Certainly not! But through their fall, to provoke them to jealousy, salvation has come to the Gentiles."

The rhetorical question that Paul now asks and responds to is one that, unfortunately, some are still erroneously asking today. The question very often takes the form of, "Is God finished with Israel? Or, "Has Israel fallen so far from God that now they are unsaveable? In essence, those of us in Jewish ministry are asked the question of whether or not we are wasting our time bringing the gospel to the Jewish people because God is finished with them.

Here in Romans 11:11, the idea of Israel stumbling must hearken us back to Romans 9:32-33, where Paul writes:

> "For they stumbled at that stumbling stone. As it is written: "Behold, I lay in Zion a stumbling stone and rock of offense, and whoever believes on Him will not be put to shame."

Salvation by grace through faith in Messiah Jesus has been a stumbling block to the majority of Jewish people who have been seeking to earn their way into heaven through the works or deeds of the Law. So, Paul's question is, "has that stumbling over Jesus, caused Israel to fall?" The Greek word translated "fall," *pésoosin,* literally means to fall prostrate, to fall dead, to become null and void. The "fall" that Paul has in mind here is one that is fatal and permanent. Has their national rejection of Jesus as their Messiah caused Israel to be dead to God once and for all? Paul's response, as in other places in Romans, is in the strongest negative possible in the Greek. Certainly not! May it never be! God forbid! Israel's fall is not final, and it is not permanent.

In the second part of Romans 11:11 Paul gives the reason for the fall:

> "But through their fall, to provoke them to jealousy, salvation has come to the Gentiles."

Here the Greek word translated "fall" is *paraptoómati,* which literally means "a false step", "a trespass," "an offense," or a "transgression", as in other translations. Paul is saying that Israel's sin of rejecting Jesus as their King Messiah did not make her "fall" final or fatal, but rather, it was a "fall" that created a wonderful opportunity for the gospel of the Jewish Messiah to be brought to the Gentile world. This would help facilitate the fulfillment of the great commission given to the Jewish disciples by Jesus in Mark 16:15, "Go into all the world and preach the gospel to every creature."

The Apostle Paul was a key component in the fulfillment of the great commission. However, he certainly wanted his new Gentile converts to understand that Israel, the Jewish people, still needed to have the gospel preached to them. "Salvation has come to the Gentiles," Paul said, but with a very important purpose and hope on his heart, that they might "provoke Israel to jealousy." This idea is not new either in Pauline thought or in this portion of Romans. Paul has already used it in Rom 10:19 when he quoted Moses from Deuteronomy 32:21:

> "I will provoke you to jealousy by those who are not a nation, I will move you to anger by a foolish nation."

Paul's heart is hopeful that somehow, as Gentiles accept Jesus the Messiah as their Savior and Lord, their lives will be so noticeably different that those Jewish people in their midst will see the change and be jealous of it. They will desire what the Gentile now has. Commenting on this verse, Mills writes:

> "Divine wisdom has used the stumbling of the Jewish nation to facilitate the preaching of the Gospel to the Gentiles. By the preaching of the Gospel, the Gentiles conversion would produce so marked a change in the life of the Gentile that the Jew would become jealous of the Gentile's change and desire that same experience take place in the life of the Jew. Nothing is so effective in preaching the Gospel as a life that has been transformed by Christ through the Holy Spirit."[59]

Some important questions must be asked at this moment, as we consider the ramifications of Paul's hope that Gentiles would somehow provoke Jewish people to jealousy for the gospel. What happened? Why did the church not take to heart the clear teaching of the Apostle to the Gentiles? Why is there so little emphasis on Jewish evangelism in the church today? If an unsaved Jewish person visited the average church service today, would he be provoked *to jealousy* and wish he had what we have—or would he just be provoked? The answers, I believe, are complex, but nevertheless readily available through church history and the Scriptures.

The early church faced strong and violent opposition from the Jewish people who were not believers. Certainly Paul attested to the kind of opposition he received from his Jewish brethren in many instances. 2 Corinthians 11:24-25 is just one example:

> "From the Jews five times I received forty stripes minus one. Three times I was beaten with rods; once I was stoned; three times I was shipwrecked; a night and a day I have been in the deep;"

What was Paul's reaction to this violent opposition? Rather than excluding them from hearing the gospel, he consistently brought the gospel message "to the Jew first." Rather than hatred and anti-semitic rhetoric, Paul brought love, and his hearts desire was to see them saved. Yet, from the early church fathers, such as Chrysostom and Augustine, to the reformers like Martin Luther, there was constant inflammatory teaching against the Jewish people. Luther, in one of his last sermons, wrote:

> "If the Jews refuse to be converted, we ought not to suffer them or bear with them any longer."[60]

It's not too difficult to see why Luther was widely quoted by Hitler as justification for the holocaust. This anti-Jewish sentiment evolved from strong Jewish opposition to the gospel, and certainly a misuse of Scriptures like Matthew 27:25, that seemed to justify Jewish persecution for their hand in Christ's death:

> "And all the people answered and said, "His blood be on us and on our children."

But beyond the response to Jewish opposition, one must not discount the spiritual warfare surrounding Jewish evangelism. Satan hates God and everything and everyone that God loves. As Israel is called, "the apple of His eye," Satan has continually tried to destroy and bring persecution against the Jewish people. It happened before Jesus was born through the likes of Pharaoh, Haman, Nebuchadnezzar, and Antiochus. It happened after Jesus died and rose, through Roman oppression, the Diaspora, the Spanish Inquisition, the Crusades, the Pogroms, and Hitler's Holocaust. Behind the scenes, doing his dirty work, inciting hatred against the Jewish people, I believe you'll find Satan, alive and active.

The Romans 11:11 model of a life lived for the Lord, so attractive and so desirable that it provokes the Jewish people to jealousy, has been an effective means of reaching the remnant over the years. To this day it is probably the most effective way to reach the Jewish people with the Gospel of Jesus the Messiah. It is the way this writer came to know Jesus as my Messiah.

I was twenty-eight years old, working for a large corporation in New York City, and as far as I know, had never met a bona-fide born-again Christian. The only professing Christians I knew, and the only Jesus I knew, was from the Roman Catholic church. Jesus to me was for the Gentiles and was hostile to Jews. He was the God of those who killed my people in the holocaust, so I was extremely anti-Christian. No life experience meeting a Christian ever caused me to think otherwise. In fact, rather than provoking me to jealousy, the action of so-called Christians provoked me to harden myself against Jesus. I married a Gentile, a Roman Catholic, but my wife and I rarely talked about spiritual things, and my love for her had nothing to do with Jesus. This was the way my life was until I met B R.

B R was my new supervisor at work. He was from a small town in Texas and spoke with a deep Texas drawl. His legal name really was B R. When he came into our office and introduced himself to me I assumed that he would be like all the other Christians in the office. In fact, since he was from the south, I assumed he would be an anti-Semite. I couldn't have been more wrong in my prejudicial assessment of B R.

Right from the very beginning I could see that there was something different about him. B R seemed to always be in a good mood. In fact, it didn't matter what time of the day or what day of the week it was, B R always seemed happy. From the time we started in the morning on Monday, until the last hour on Friday, B R had a smile on his face and was friendly and outgoing to everyone. What a contrast to the rest of us, who could barely survive the day, let alone be constantly in a good mood. The contrast was so strong, that we teased B R and asked him if he did drugs to keep himself in such a good mood all the time.

In my office people used a lot of curse words to pepper our speech. We never, however, heard a bad word come out of B R's mouth. In fact, eventually we stopped using foul language around him because he would chide us for using it and encourage us to stop. People did a lot of gossiping around the office, bad-mouthing others in order to climb up the corporate ladder. B R wouldn't tolerate gossip and he would often tell us to go to another person if we had something against them. We all were beginning to wonder how it was possible for someone to be that good.

There was one trait, however, that really got my attention. It was the incredible peacefulness and calmness that B R exuded. Nothing ever seemed to rattle him. No matter how stressful the situation at work was, no matter how difficult the circumstances became, B R always had it together. There was something about his life that was special and appealing, and I found myself becoming envious of B R. One day, while we were having lunch together, I finally got the courage to ask him, "What is it about you that's so different from anyone else?" I told him that he obviously had something in his life that I didn't have and I wanted to know what it was. His response to me was surprising in that he asked me if I was sure I wanted to hear the answer. When I told him I was sure, he invited me back to his office. It was there that B R gave me the answer to my question.

When B R told me to close the door to his office and sit in front of his desk, I wondered what was coming next. B R opened a drawer in his desk and took out the largest Bible I had ever seen, and slammed it down on his desk. He said to me, "This is what makes me different." "I read the Word of God every day." "Jesus Christ is my Lord and Savior." At that point I thought to myself, "good grief, what have I unleashed?" But then he said something to me no one had ever said before. He said to me that Jesus was the Jewish Messiah, the one we were waiting for. Before he could say anything else I interrupted him. I said, "Listen B R, Jesus isn't the Messiah. My people have been murdered because of Jesus. If He was the Messiah there would be peace in the world, and there certainly isn't peace. So, if you want to stay my friend, you'll never tell me that stuff again."

B R never shared about Jesus with me again. He didn't have to. Despite the fact that I discounted what he said, I couldn't discount that his life provoked me to jealousy. I knew he had something that I didn't have. God took that seed that B R planted in my heart and used my wonderful Gentile wife, who became a believer, to lead me to faith in Jesus. But what started the process was the faithfulness of a Gentile man who took seriously the charge in Romans 11:11:

> "But through their fall, to provoke them to jealousy,
> salvation has come to the Gentiles."

Romans 11:11 can be considered to be the Gentile Great Commission. The original Great Commission was the risen Jesus speaking to His Jewish disciples telling them to bring the message of the Jewish Messiah to the Gentiles. This was then passed down to the church, which in the beginning was virtually all Jewish and needed some intervention from God to move out into the Gentile world with the message of the Jewish Messiah. Now Paul, speaking to primarily Gentile believers, is saying, you need to bring the message of Jesus, the gospel, back to the original messengers. You need to provoke the Jewish people to jealousy by living the kind of life that would cause others to take notice. The challenge for every Gentile believer is how do you measure up?

As Paul continues the thought of Romans 11:11 in Romans 11:12-15, he elaborates upon the benefit that would accrue to Gentiles as more and more Jewish people come to faith in their Messiah. He wants his Gentile readers to recognize for themselves the significance of Israel's restoration to divine favor, which will be shown and illustrated by the growth of the believing remnant:

> "Now if their fall is riches for the world, and their failure riches for the Gentiles, how much more their fullness! For I speak to you Gentiles; inasmuch as I am an apostle to the Gentiles, I magnify my ministry, if by any means I may provoke to jealousy those who are my flesh and save some of them. For if their being cast away is the reconciling of the world, what will their acceptance be but life from the dead?"

The two words Paul uses in v. 12 to describe national Israel's rejection of Jesus as their Messiah is "fall" and "failure." "Fall" as in 11:11 is the Greek word *parȧptooma,* which can also be translated transgression or trespass, as in other translations. "Failure" is the Greek word *heétteema,* which literally means deterioration or loss. Israel's transgression in rejecting Jesus as Messiah has been, for her, a great failure, the loss of incredible privilege and blessing. If Israel's rejection of Jesus has resulted in humankind, the world, being incredibly blessed, and the Gentiles now being possessors of such great spiritual blessings, think of how much greater blessings Israel's fullness will bring. In order to understand this last statement, the phrase, "Israel's fullness," must be analyzed.

The Greek word *pleérooma*, translated "fullness", has both a quantitative as well as a qualitative sense to the word. In the quantitative sense, the word "fullness" would have to do with the "full number" of Jews who are to get saved. This is thought to be the sense of the word, by many scholars in Romans 11:25, when it speaks of the Gentiles:

> "For I do not desire, brethren, that you should be ignorant of this mystery, lest you should be wise in your own opinion, that blindness in part has happened to Israel until the fullness of the Gentiles has come in."

Moo commenting on this writes:

> "The implication in this case would be that to the present remnant there will be added a much greater number of Jewish believers so as to "fill up" the number of Jews destined for salvation."[61]

But, I believe Paul is thinking much more than mere numbers. Rather the word should be understood in its qualitative sense as fulfillment (NAS), or completion, and refers to the full restoration to Israel of the blessings of God that she is now, in her current state, not partaking of. Mills commenting on this writes,:

> "'The whole creation groaneth and travaileth in pain until' (Romans 8:22) the day of Israel's restoration. What joy, what blessing, what exultation the restoration of Israel will bring to pass! If being the 'tail' of the nations has blessed so many individual Gentiles, how much greater will the blessings be when Israel becomes the 'head'? (Deuteronomy 28:13) Scripture gives us the answer and we need not speculate. Peace will be universal; there will be no more hostilities; there will be no need for politics; and there will be no crimes committed. There will be one law, and one Law-giver seated at Jerusalem. There will be holy demonstrations; Israel will be the spiritual ministers in this kingdom; '...and the lion shall eat straw like the ox' (Isaiah 11:7)[62]

After this series of blessings Paul now makes specific application to his own ministry in Rom 11:13-14:

> "For I speak to you Gentiles; inasmuch as I am an apostle to the Gentiles, I magnify my ministry, if by any means I may provoke to jealousy those who are my flesh and save some of them."

It is the Gentile's role in Jewish evangelism that is the jumping off point for Paul's remarks about his own ministry. As Apostle to the Gentiles, Paul may be concerned about correcting any misunderstanding on the part of his predominantly Gentile readers in Rome about his concern for their part in Jewish evangelism. Some may be asking the question, "if Paul, who is Jewish, is the Apostle to the Gentiles, why should we Gentiles go to the Jews with the gospel?" Paul's response to this is that as the Apostle to the Gentiles his ministry is magnified, when Gentiles get saved, then live exemplary lives, thereby provoking Jewish people to jealousy and to believe in Jesus as Messiah. Paul is certainly not saying that it is the only reason that he is involved in this ministry to the Gentiles nor that it is even the most important reason for his ministry. Rather, his purpose here is to show that it is clearly a motivating factor in his work among the Gentiles. His heart's desire is still that his Jewish brethren would be saved. Moo, commenting on this writes:

> "Paul's hope that his preaching to Gentiles will have a positive impact on Jews is based on the "jealousy" theme that he introduced in v. 11b. As God uses Paul's preaching to bring more and more Gentiles to salvation, Paul hopes that his own "flesh and blood" will become jealous and seek for themselves the blessings of this salvation."[63]

With Romans 11:15, Paul returns to the question of what the implication of Israel as a nation returning to God through their Messiah will be:

> "For if their being cast away is the reconciling of the world, what will their acceptance be but life from the dead?"

The phrase, "cast away," the Greek word *apoboleé,* is also translated in other versions "rejected." It literally means "a throwing away or loss." This is equivalent to the words "fall" and "failure" in verse 12. This casting away, this rejection of Israel, this unbelief of the majority of the nation, resulted in the gospel preached to the Gentiles, which brought reconciliation to the world. Witmer, commenting on this, writes:

> "Paul reminded his Gentile readers that Israel's rejection meant the reconciliation of the world in the purpose of God. Because Israel rejected Christ, the gospel was taken to these Gentiles. In Scripture reconciliation is a work of God in the death of Christ which does not *actually* restore an individual to fellowship with God but provides the basis for him to be restored to fellowship (cf. 2 Cor. 5:18-20). This statement serves to explain the meaning of the phrases "riches for the world" and "riches for the Gentiles" in Romans 11:12. When a person comes to Christ by faith, God's work of reconciliation is appropriated to him and he then has fellowship with God and the spiritual enmity is removed."[64]

Paul moves on from what the impact of Israel's rejection of the gospel meant to the Gentile world to what the impact of Israel's acceptance of the gospel would be. He asks in Romans

11:15, "What will their acceptance be but life from the dead?" The Greek word translated "acceptance," *prósleempsis,* is also translated as "receiving" in other versions, going with the idea of God casting away and God receiving back to Himself. This is the equivalent of what Paul called "their fullness," in Romans 11:12. What happens to the world when Israel as a nation returns to their Lord? These greater riches he refers to in v. 12 relating to their fullness he now describes as "life from the dead." This is an important statement and we need to answer the question, what does he mean by that?

Commentators tend to hold to two different views regarding this statement. The first view is a literal view, that we can take the statement, "life from the dead," literally, understanding it to mean the general resurrection that will take place after the return of Christ in glory. Stott writes:

> "Thus the conversion of Israel will be the signal for the resurrection, the last stage of the eschatological process initiated by the death and resurrection of Jesus."[65]

The second view is a spiritual view, that we can take the statement, "life from the dead," as referring to unprecedented and unimaginable blessings that will enrich the Gentiles, likely to be an unprecedented spiritual revival that takes place in the world. In this view it is thought Paul is saying, if the world receives incredible blessings when the majority of Israel is rebelling against God and rejects the gospel, just imagine what the blessings will be like when Israel returns to God and is obedient to Him. Advocates of this view often point to the phrase about the prodigal son's return in Luke 15:24, "for this my son was dead and is alive again; he was lost and is found."

It seems more likely that what Paul has in view here is a more literal "life from the dead," focusing on the last days. It will be in those days, when the majority of Israel comes to believe that Jesus is Messiah that there will truly be "life from the dead." A great worldwide revival in the final days will take place and it will be led by the 144,000 Jewish evangelists described in Revelation 7. Moo concludes by writing:

> "Therefore, as Israel's 'trespass' (vv. 11-12) and 'rejection' (v. 15) trigger the stage of salvation history in which Paul (and we) are located, a stage in which God is

specially blessing Gentiles, so Israel's 'fullness' (v.12) and 'acceptance' (v.15) will trigger the climactic end of salvation history. Paul insists on the vital, continuing significance of Israel in salvation history, against tendencies among Gentile Christians to discard Israel from any further role in the plan of God."[66]

CHAPTER 10

A Wild Olive Branch That Is Grafted In

In this next sermon section, Paul begins, in Romans 11:16-18, by using two metaphors, one taken from Israeli custom and the other from agriculture, both intended to justify Paul's confidence in the abundance of blessings to the world, through Israel's return to God, as described in vvs 11-15:

> "For if the firstfruit is holy, the lump is also holy; and if the root is holy, so are the branches. And if some of the branches were broken off, and you, being a wild olive tree, were grafted in among them, and with them became a partaker of the root and fatness of the olive tree, do not boast against the branches. But if you do boast, remember that you do not support the root, but the root supports you."

The first illustration is from Numbers 15:17-21 after Israel entered the promised land and had their first wheat harvest:

> "Again the LORD spoke to Moses, saying, "Speak to the children of Israel, and say to them: 'When you come into the land to which I bring you, then it will be, when you eat of the bread of the land, that you shall offer up a heave offering to the LORD. You shall offer up a cake of the first of your ground meal as a heave offering; as a heave offering of the threshing floor, so shall you offer it up. Of the first of your ground meal you shall give to the LORD a heave offering throughout your generations."

The first part of the dough was to be offered up to God as a sign that the entire lump belonged to Him. The same concept was seen in the Feast of First Fruits, when the priest offered a sheaf to the Lord as a token that the entire harvest belonged to Him. (Leviticus. 23:9-14). Again, the basic idea is that when God accepts the part, He sanctifies the whole.

Applying this to Israel's history, Paul's argument becomes clear. When God accepted the founder of the nation, the patriarch Abraham, in so doing He set apart his descendants as well. God accepted the other patriarchs, Isaac and Jacob, in spite of their sins or failings, and certainly there were many. Paul's conclusion, applying to Israel, means that the part can convey holiness to the whole. Writing about the remnant, Moo states:

> "It reinforces the hope for a spiritual renewal of Israel that vv. 11-15 have implied; the holiness of "part" of Israel is good reason to anticipate a "fullness" and "acceptance" for the whole of Israel."[67]

Mills writes of this as well:

> "Out of the loins of Abraham, who was the 'firstfruit' and the 'root,'the nation Israel came into existence. God set Abraham and his seed, Israel, apart. They are God's peculiar possession. Abraham was that peculiar "firstfruit that God chose for Himself. In the same manner God chose Israel for Himself."[68]

The second illustration, parallel to the first, is that of the Olive Tree taken from Jeremiah 11:16 and Hosea 14:6. The Olive Tree is a symbol of the nation of Israel. Paul was not discussing the relationship of individual believers to God, but the place of Israel in the plan of God. The roots of the tree are what supports the tree. Again, the roots are a symbol of the patriarchs who founded the nation. God made His covenants with Abraham, Isaac, and Jacob and He will not deny them or change them. Thus, it is God's promise to Abraham and the patriarchs that sustains Israel even today.

Now in a new image, Paul restates the tragedy of Romans 9-11 over which he is heartbroken. Many of the Jewish people, as Paul has emphasized, did not believe in Jesus as the Messiah. Paul pictures them here as being branches broken off of the tree. However, Paul also sees an amazing thing taking place: other branches were grafted into the tree to share in the life of the tree. These new branches were the Gentiles, branches that come from a "wild olive tree." Paul says of these branches in Romans 11:17, "and with them became a partaker of the root and fatness of the olive tree."

It is very important to note that these branches were grafted in among them, among the remnant of Jewish believers, not instead of them. These new Gentile believers did not replace the remnant of Israel, but rather found themselves among them, bearing fruit with them. This is a further elaboration of what Paul has said in Romans 11:5 and 7: that there was a faithful remnant of Israel, a remnant of Jewish believers who were bearing fruit. It was that faithful remnant which brought the good news of the Messiah of Israel to the Gentiles. Now, those new Gentile believers are grafted in among them, partaking of all of the goodness of the tree. Mills, commenting on this, writes:

> "The Gentile at his conversion was spiritually grafted into the good olive tree and became a part-taker, not an all-taker, with the Jewish believers. Jewish and Gentile believer became one. They partook of the root, Abraham, (Romans 4), and of the fatness (of the righteousness which is by faith, Romans 4:3) of the good olive tree."[69]

This process, Paul will tell us later on in 11:24, was contrary to nature. Usually a cultivated branch is grafted into a wild tree and shares its life without producing its poor fruit. In this case, though, it was the wild branch that was grafted into the good tree. This speaks volumes of the supernatural power of God and His love for all people. Mills adds:

> "God is a super-natural God. He takes the wild branch and cuts it off the wild tree (the Gentile) and grafts it into the good tree (Israel) among the good branches. Even though it is a wild branch, God performs a miracle and the wild branch bears the same fruit as the good branch; in fact, both produce fruit unto God (Romans 7:4). Thus the Gentile receives the blessings of God through the Jew."[70]

Now, in this church age, Gentile believers have privileges that Jewish unbelievers do not have. Grafted into the Olive Tree, they are partaking of blessings that were at one time only for Israel, for the Jewish people. Sadly, rather than looking at the unbelieving Jewish people with the same compassion that Paul has, longing for their return to God, the history of the church, since the writing of the book of Romans, has been marked by anti-Semitism and hatred. They did not heed Paul's warning in Rom 11:18:

> "do not boast against the branches. But if you do boast, remember that you do not support the root, but the root supports you."

These Gentile believers appear to have come to the conclusion that not only have the doors of salvation been opened up to them in an unprecedented way, but also that the same doors of salvation have been closed to those of Israel not part of the remnant, the Jewish people who weren't believers. That belief in the closed door to the Jewish people was cause for both anti-semitic tendencies in the church, as well as a diminishing of and movement away from the Jewish roots of Christianity. Moo writes:

> "Gentile Christians who boast over Jews are demonstrating an attitude of disdain for the Jewish heritage. Yet it is that very heritage upon which the Gentile Christian themselves depend for their spiritual standing. For "the root" that gives spiritual nourishment to Jewish and Gentile believers alike is the patriarchs as recipients and transmitters of the promises of God. And that root is not only of historical interest. As the present tense that Paul uses here indicates, the root of the patriarchs continue to be the source of spiritual nourishment that believers require."[71]

Anticipating some Gentile believers seeking to justify their feelings of superiority over the plight of the Jews, Paul now addresses a hypothetical line of argument in Romans 11:19-20:

> "You will say then, "Branches were broken off that I might be grafted in. Well said. Because of unbelief they were broken off, and you stand by faith. Do not be haughty, but fear."

Perhaps the Gentile Christian believes God loves them more now. Perhaps they believe that they are more righteous and therefore more deserving of salvation than the Jews. Paul does not get into the validity of the argument only with the reality of the facts. When he says, "Well said," he's referring to the fact that the natural branch, unbelieving Jewish people, were broken off because of their unbelief, and Gentiles were grafted in because of their faith in Jesus. But rather than boasting in that, rather than being prideful and haughty in that, the Gentile Christian should have an attitude of fear and reverence. Moo comments:

"Paul also argues that this salvation is, in turn, designed to stimulate Jews to jealousy as the means of their spiritual restoration. God's purposes in "cutting off" natural branches extend far beyond the inclusion of Gentiles. It is the egotism of Gentile Christians, who present God's manifold plan as having the salvation of themselves as its focus, that Paul wishes to expose and criticize."[72]

Paul explains the reason the Gentile believers should fear in Romans 11:21. "For if God did not spare the natural branches, He may not spare you either." Paul warned the Gentiles that they were obligated to Israel since they were attached to the tree and dependent upon the roots. Therefore they dared not boast of their new spiritual position, but rather ought to be striving to live such incredible lives that they would be provoking Israel to jealousy. The Gentiles entered into God's salvation because of faith, and not because of anything good they had done. Paul here was discussing the Gentiles collectively, and not the individual experience of one believer or another. Warren Wiersbe writes:

"It is worth noting that, according to Bible prophecy, the professing Gentile church will be "cut off" because of apostasy. First Timothy 4 and 2 Timothy 3, along with 2 Thessalonians 2, all indicate that the professing church in the last days will depart from the faith. *There is no hope for the apostate church, but there is hope for apostate Israel*! Why? Because of the roots of the olive tree. God will keep His promises to the patriarchs, but God will break off the Gentiles because of their unbelief."[73]

In verses 22-24, Paul concludes this discussion of the olive tree, by stating how logical it is that God would be able to graft the natural branch back into the tree if he is able to graft the wild branches in:

"Therefore consider the goodness and severity of God: on those who fell, severity; but toward you, goodness, if you continue in His goodness. Otherwise you also will be cut off. And they also, if they do not continue in unbelief, will be grafted in, for God is able to graft them in again. For if you were cut out of the olive tree which is wild by nature, and were grafted contrary to nature into a

> cultivated olive tree, how much more will these, who
> are natural branches, be grafted into their own olive tree?"

Paul here summarizes his whole discussion of God's sovereign choice in temporarily setting aside national Israel and proclaiming righteousness by faith to all who will believe. When Paul writes, "Therefore consider," he's saying, based on what you've heard up to this point you need to take a particularly close look at both "the goodness and severity of God." The Greek word translated "goodness," *chreestóteeta,* means also kindness, gentleness and generosity. The Greek word translated "severity," *apotomían,* means also to cut off or shear, or to fall from a height. Romans 11:24 is the only time this word is used in the New Testament.

God's sovereign choice involved severity toward those of Israel who fell in unbelief, but that same decision displayed the goodness of God toward the new Gentile converts. God's continuing His goodness to the Gentiles depends on their continuing in His goodness. If Gentiles do not continue or persist in God's goodness, they also will be cut off. God's goodness cannot be abused or taken for granted. It is not a license for sin. The Gentiles are warned by Paul to carefully consider what happened to Israel, as they repeatedly refused to heed the warnings of God through His prophets. Those unbelieving branches in Israel had to be broken off. If the Gentiles do the same as Israel did, Paul is warning them to expect the same.

Paul is not suggesting here that a Christian can lose his salvation; but rather he's referring to Gentiles as a whole turning from the gospel much as Israel as a nation had done. As Wiersbe discussed, this has already happened historically. Paul has been stressing the equality of both Jew and Gentile in God's sight. Just as those in Israel who did not believe are "cut off," so too the Gentiles who do not continue in God's goodness will be "cut off."

Now, in Romans 11:23-24, Paul uses this same principle of equality to offer hope for the future, and discusses the possibility of unbelieving Israel returning to God.

> "And they also, if they do not continue in unbelief,
> will be grafted in, for God is able to graft them in again.
> For if you were cut out of the olive tree which is wild by

nature, and were grafted contrary to nature into a cultivated olive tree, how much more will these, who are natural branches, be grafted into their own olive tree?"

One can't help but think of the promises God made to the patriarchs and the prophets, beginning even with Moses, regarding Israel's physical and spiritual blessings. All of those blessings will come to pass, and unbelieving Israel will return to the Lord just as the prophet Jeremiah writes in Jeremiah 31:33-34:

> "But this is the covenant that I will make with the house of Israel after those days, says the LORD: I will put My law in their minds, and write it on their hearts; and I will be their God, and they shall be My people. No more shall every man teach his neighbor, and every man his brother, saying, 'Know the LORD,' for they all shall know Me, from the least of them to the greatest of them, says the LORD. For I will forgive their iniquity, and their sin I will remember no more."

There will come a time when Israel will turn back to God and those natural branches will be grafted back in. Paul's wording in Romans 11:24 emphasizes that truth. He uses the same verb in the same mood and tense in v. 24 for "be grafted into," as in v. 23, "shall be grafted in." The God who is able to supernaturally graft "wild branches" into a cultivated olive tree, something that is contrary to nature, will certainly be able to graft back into the tree "natural branches" that were broken off. The importance of this truth of the restoration of Israel should not go unnoticed. Mills adds:

> "If God has cast away Israel and will not restore her to her national position and possession; if God will not keep His promises which He made to the patriarchs and their posterity (Israel); if God is not bound by His own word in the Old Testament, then by the same token God is not bound by His own word in the New Testament. It is the same God that speaks and acts in both Testaments. If God can cast away Israel to eternal dissolution, never again to become the chosen nation under God's protective care; if God can do this with Israel, then God will not keep His promises to His New Testament saints. What other assurance has a saint?"[74]

God is not finished with the Jewish people. The church has not replaced Israel. Paul will bring this all to conclusion with Romans 11:25ff, as he will show God's restoration of Israel and the Jewish people. Witmer, concluding his teaching on this section, writes:

> "The "olive tree" is not the church; it is the spiritual stock of Abraham. Believing Gentiles are included in that sphere of blessing so that in the Church Age both Jews and Gentiles are in Christ's body (Ephesians 2:11-22; 3:6). Yet someday Israel as a whole will turn to Christ (as Paul discussed in Rom. 11:25-27). This passage does not teach that the national promises to Israel have been abrogated and are now being fulfilled by the church. This idea, taught by amillenarians, is foreign to Paul's point, for he said Israel's fall is temporary. While believing Gentiles share in the blessings of the Abrahamic Covenant (Genseis 12:3b) as Abraham's spiritual children (Galatians 3:8-9), they do not permanently replace Israel as the heirs of God's promises (Genesis 12:2-3; 15:18-21; 17:19-21; 22:15-18)."[75]

The church, historically, has misunderstood much of what Paul was trying to teach here in this section of Romans 11. Replacement theology has often been the dominant view of Israel in the church. It is contrary to what Paul was trying to teach the church at Rome and by extension everyone who reads the book of Romans. Paul clearly makes a distinction between Israel and the Church here in Romans but in other places as well, especially Ephesians. Moo concludes his teaching on this section by writing:

> "What is particularly pernicious in the "replacement" model is the assumption so easily made that "church" = Gentiles. This assumption was apparently beginning to be made by Paul's contemporaries. And it has certainly been embraced by many Christians throughout history, contributing (albeit often inadvertently) to the anti-Semitism that has too often stained the name of Christ. We must not become so focused on the theology of Paul's teaching here that we miss its purpose: to criticize those who are Gentiles for arrogance toward believing and unbelieving Jews and to remind us that our own spiritual heritage is a Jewish one."[76]

CHAPTER 11

All Israel Will Be Saved

The final sermon section of Romans 9-11 begins with Paul, having completed his illustration of the "olive tree," now addressing his readers directly once again, beginning in Romans 11:25:

> "For I do not desire, brethren, that you should be ignorant of this mystery, lest you should be wise in your own opinion, that blindness in part has happened to Israel until the fullness of the Gentiles has come in."

The word "For" at the beginning of v. 25 ties what is to follow with what has preceded. He has been writing to Gentile believers regarding the future of Israel as it pertains to her relationship to God through Jesus the Messiah. Now in the verses to follow Paul is going to be quite specific in what is going to take place. The Greek word translated "ignorant," *agnoeín,* literally means "not to know." Paul wants to be certain in his writing to Gentile believers that there is no ignorance on their part, no lack of knowledge, no misinformation regarding a mystery he's about to elaborate on. The reason for this is that they would be less likely to have an attitude of conceit and superiority toward the Jewish people, less likely to be "wise in your own opinion."

In Scripture, a mystery is not a truth that is difficult to understand, but rather a truth previously unrevealed which is now revealed and publicly proclaimed. Paul uses the word mystery in other portions of Scripture. In Ephesians 3:9, Paul describes "The Church," Jew and Gentile, as the body of Christ, as a mystery; and also in 1 Corinthians 15:51 Paul describes "The Rapture of the Church" as a mystery. The mystery that Paul reveals here is …"that blindness in part has happened to Israel until the fullness of the Gentiles has come in."

The mystery was not that there was a "blindness in part," or "partial hardening" (NASB, NIV), of Israel, as this was something that was clearly known and understood by the believers. What was not known, however, was just how long that blindness or hardening would last. Obviously some, perhaps many, thought that it would be permanent. With the word "until," Paul now reveals the mystery. The blindness in part would not be permanent, it would cease when "the fullness of the Gentiles has come in." A proper interpretation of this phrase is critical to ascertain what Paul is revealing here.

As already discussed, there is both a qualitative as well as a quantitative aspect to the word "fullness." Certainly the translators of the NIV show that they believe the phrase should be understood as quantitative when they translate it, "until the full number of the Gentiles has come in." The majority of commentators seem to favor this view, that the partial hardening of Israel will end when the last Gentile comes to faith in Jesus the Messiah. They believe that God has a predetermined number of Gentiles that are going to be saved and when that number is reached the partial hardening will be removed. Another variation to this quantitative view is that the "fullness of the Gentiles" refers to the end of the church age, when the last Gentile in that age is saved, then, the hardening or blindness will be lifted. I believe the evidence leads to a different conclusion.

I believe the phrase, "the fullness of the Gentiles," here in Romans 11:25, should be understood qualitatively, to be synonymous with the phrase, "the times of the Gentiles," in Luke 21:24, "And Jerusalem will be trampled by Gentiles until the times of the Gentiles are fulfilled." The "times of the Gentiles," in Luke 21:24, refers to the time Israel is under Gentile domination, and relates to the Seventy Weeks of Daniel in 9:24-27. Therefore, the phrase, "until the fullness of the Gentiles comes in," should be understood as the end of the seventieth week, the end of the tribulation period, then the "blindness in part," the "partial hardening," will be lifted. Mills writes,

> "It is interesting to note the Rabbis taught the truth that Israel would experience "the time of Jacob's trouble" before the Messiah comes -- "When thou shalt see the time in which many troubles shall come like a river upon Israel, then expect the Messiah himself."
> (Tract, Sanhedrin f98:1)"[77]

The consequence of the "blindness in part" being lifted is seen in Rom 11:26-27:

> "And so all Israel will be saved, as it is written: 'The Deliverer will come out of Zion, And He will turn away ungodliness from Jacob; For this is My covenant with them, When I take away their sins.'

The Greek phrase, *kaí hoútoos,* translated "and so," should be taken to mean "in consequence of this," denoting that it comes about because of Israel's "blindness in part" ending. Therefore, Paul's statement can be understood to say, "As a consequence of the blindness in part ending, when the fullness of the Gentiles comes in, all Israel will be saved." "All Israel will be saved" is a statement that has historically been filled with controversy. What did Paul mean when he said it? It would be helpful to eliminate, first of all, what it doesn't mean.

"All Israel will be saved" does not mean that every Jewish person who has ever lived is going to be in heaven with God because they are Jewish. Those holding to a double covenant position would say that because of the Abrahamic covenant, Jewish people will be saved apart from Jesus. This heretical position has already been discussed. Neither does "all Israel will be saved" mean that Israel is now the church, true believers, and Paul is merely reiterating the fact that it is the church, the true believers who are saved. This is not affirming "replacement theology." Paul clearly teaches that there is a distinction between Israel and the church, having used the term "Israel" ten times in Romans 9-11, with each referring to ethnic Israel.

Many commentators hold to the position that "all Israel will be saved" is referring to the elect remnant within Israel. The problem with this position is that Paul is revealing a mystery in Romans 11:25 regarding the lifting of the partial blindness or hardening of Israel, whose consequence is that "all Israel will be saved." He has already discussed the remnant of Israel, the elect, and this then would not be something new. Even those who say that this is talking about the remnant growing to a larger number do not deal with the issue of "all Israel." So then what does Paul mean?

While the phrase "all Israel" can refer to national Israel, the vast majority and not every individual, as some teach, I believe Paul, when using the Greek phrase *pás Israeél,* uses it in its most literal sense, meaning every one of Israel. What Paul has in mind is every one in Israel alive at the time of Jesus' return, recognizing Him as Messiah and getting saved. The event itself is prophecied by the prophet Zechariah in 12:10 and 13:1:

> "And I will pour on the house of David and on the inhabitants of Jerusalem the Spirit of grace and supplication; then they will look on Me whom they pierced. Yes, they will mourn for Him as one mourns for his only son, and grieve for Him as one grieves for a firstborn."
>
> "In that day a fountain shall be opened for the house of David and for the inhabitants of Jerusalem, for sin and for uncleanness.

What the prophet pictures here is the awesome return of Jesus to earth. At the end of the "Great Tribulation," the nations of the world, under the leadership of the Anti-Christ, will be gathered against Israel to destroy her once and for all. Zechariah describes it in 14:1-2:

> "Behold, the day of the LORD is coming, and your spoil will be divided in your midst. For I will gather all the nations to battle against Jerusalem; the city shall be taken, the houses rifled, and the women ravished. Half of the city shall go into captivity, but the remnant of the people shall not be cut off from the city."

The Lord will then return, along with the glorified church, to rescue Israel and ultimately save them from their sins. Zechariah writes, in 14:3-5:

> "Then the LORD will go forth and fight against those nations, As He fights in the day of battle. And in that day His feet will stand on the Mount of Olives, which faces Jerusalem on the east. And the Mount of Olives shall be split in two, from east to west, making a very large valley; half of the mountain shall move toward the north and half of it toward the south. Then you shall flee through My mountain valley, for the mountain valley shall reach to Azal. Yes, you shall flee as you fled from the earthquake in the days of Uzziah king of Judah. Thus the LORD my God will come, And all the saints with You.

The people of Israel will see Jesus standing on the Mount of Olives. They will see their pierced Messiah, recognize Him as the Promised One, and accept Him as their Savior. Their response will be great mourning, as Zechariah writes, "they will mourn for Him as one mourns for his only son." The reason there is such great mourning is the terrible cost this national rejection of the Messiah has been to Israel.

Zechariah 13:8-9 describes the fact that the loss of life will be staggering during this time:

> "And it shall come to pass in all the land," says the LORD, "That two-thirds in it shall be cut off and die, but one-third shall be left in it: I will bring the one-third through the fire, will refine them as silver is refined, and test them as gold is tested. They will call on My name, and I will answer them. I will say, 'This is My people'; and each one will say, 'The LORD is my God.'"

It is the one-third who survive, the one-third whom God brings through the fire, the one-third alive when Jesus returns, who see Him and recognize Him as the Messiah and are saved. This is the group of whom Paul is speaking in Romans 11:26 when he says, "And so all Israel will be saved."

Right after Paul makes the statement "all Israel will be saved", he quotes, with a bit of variation, from Isaiah 59:20-21 and 27:9, which, as he's done in other sections of Romans 9-11, serves to reinforce his teaching.

> And so all Israel will be saved, as it is written: "The Deliverer will come out of Zion, and He will turn away ungodliness from Jacob; For this is My covenant with them, when I take away their sins."

Commenting on these verses, Stott writes,

> "These verses together make three affirmations. First, '*the deliverer will come from Zion.*' This was, in Isaiah's original, a reference to Christ's first coming. Secondly, what he would do when he came was described in moral terms; he would *turn 'godlessness away from Jacob.'* This seems to be an allusion to Isaiah 27:9, where Jacob's guilt would be atoned for and removed. Thirdly, the deliverer would establish God's covenant, which promised the forgiveness of sins. Putting these truths together, the deliverer would come to bring his people to repentance and so to forgiveness, according to God's covenant promise.

It is clear from this that the 'salvation' of Israel for which Paul has prayed (10:1), to which he will lead his own people by arousing their envy (11:14), which has also come to the Gentiles (11:11), and which one day 'all Israel' will experience (11:26), is salvation from sin through faith in Jesus Christ."[78]

There is no possibility given here or in any of the writings of Paul for there to be any other way for a Jewish person to get saved apart from Jesus. The truth of the Scriptures must be our basis for action despite the fact, especially since the holocaust, that there has been an outcry from Jewish groups demanding Christian missionary activity cease, as well as a subtle equating of Jewish evangelism with anti-semitism. There is no other way for anyone, Jew or Gentile, to be saved. As Jesus Himself said in John 14:6:

"I am the way, the truth, and the life. No one comes to the Father except through Me."

Much of the church in the post holocaust era has sought to be loving and inoffensive to the Jewish people by not evangelizing them. In so doing, it has, in the guise of avoiding anti-semitism, advocated a position which absolutely has to be regarded as anti-semitic. What can be more hateful than withholding the message of Jesus to any people group, let alone the people group through whom Jesus came. The church needs to see the priority of Jewish evangelism from the heart of the Apostle Paul. When they do, the question of whether or not it's appropriate to bring the Gospel to the Jewish people will no longer be considered. Commenting on this Dunn writes:

"Paul was not thinking in terms of what we normally call conversion from one religion to another but of the recognition by Jews of the final and true form of their own religion."[79]

Paul begins his conclusion on this teaching about God's program for Israel in Romans 11:28:

"Concerning the gospel they are enemies for your sake, but concerning the election they are beloved for the sake of the fathers."

Share with a Jewish person your belief that Jesus the Messiah is the only way to God the Father, and the likely response you're going to get is hostility, anger, belligerence and antagonism. There is an active and passive voice to the phrase "Concerning the gospel they are enemies." It is likely Paul has both in mind here. Passive having to do with Jewish people having been blinded, hardened, and rejected by God. Active having to do with their being disobedient, unbelieving, and stubborn regarding the gospel of Jesus the Messiah. Notice though, as Paul is writing to Gentile believers, that he says, "they are enemies *for your sake*." He is reminding them of what he said in Romans 11:11:

> "But through their fall, to provoke them to jealousy, salvation has come to the Gentiles."

But rather than taking that calling to provoke Israel to jealousy seriously, historically the Gentile church has written off the Jewish people as enemies of God, no longer savable. Mills writes:

> "If blindness and hardness of heart had not been placed upon the Jews, the Gentiles would not have the opportunity that they now have to hear the gospel. The problem today, and it has been for centuries, is that some Gentile Christians have gone to extremes in claiming that the Jews have been, and still are, excluded from the gospel. These Gentile Christians claim that the Jews have had their chance. How foolish and wild this idea is in light of the clear teaching of Scripture!"[80]

Having discussed Israel's position concerning the gospel as enemies for the sake of the Gentiles, Paul, in the second half of Romans 11:28, discusses Israel's position concerning their election. He writes, "but concerning the election they are beloved for the sake of the fathers." What does Paul mean by "concerning the election?" Some say that this is referring to the believing remnant of Israel, distinguishing believing Israel within the nation. This doesn't really fit the context. Rather, I believe it is referring to their election as a nation, as God's Chosen People. The phrase "for the sake of the fathers," refers to the covenants God made with the patriarchs, Abraham, Isaac, and Jacob. Stott writes regarding this:

> "The Jews are the chosen, special people of God, the descendants of the noble patriarchs with whom the covenant was made, and to whom the promises were given. So then, in relation to election, and for the sake of the patriarchs (because God is faithful to his covenants and promises), he loves them and is determined to bring them to salvation."[81]

When the Lord made promises in His covenant with Abraham, affirming that covenant with Isaac and Jacob, He promised to bless Israel as a nation, make Israel a blessing to the world, and give them a land as an everlasting inheritance. While these promises have in part come to pass, with Israel multiplying as a nation and the world blessed through Israel's Messiah Jesus, the promises of land have not been brought to pass because of her disobedience. The promises to Abraham will not be complete, until Israel is in the promised land and is in right relationship with her God through the Messiah. That won't happen until Jesus returns to the earth, but Paul makes it clear that it will eventually happen when he writes in Rom 11:29, "For the gifts and the calling of God are irrevocable."

Israel still has a place in God's plan because God is a faithful God. God's promises to Israel, and God's calling of Israel, cannot be taken back or changed, or God would cease to be God. This is exactly what Moses was writing about in Num 23:19,

> "God is not a man, that He should lie, nor a son of man, that He should repent. Has He said, and will He not do? Or has He spoken, and will He not make it good?"

The fact that Israel may not be currently enjoying her blessings or living up to her privileges as a chosen people, does not affect this fact one bit. God will be consistent with Himself and true to His Word no matter what people may do. Because of who He is, His promises are irrevocable. What a phenomenal blessing to every believer. We can take all the incredible promises God's made to us and hold on to them as being absolutely sure to happen. And one of the most important reasons we can do this is what Paul is teaching here, that God's promises to Israel will all take place.

In Romans 11:30-32, Paul concludes his teaching on God's plan for Israel and the Gentiles by reminding the Gentiles of their previous plight before becoming believers, and how God has brought the gospel to them that in turn they might help lead Israel back to their God.

> "For as you were once disobedient to God, yet have now obtained mercy through their disobedience, even so these also have now been disobedient, that through the mercy shown you they also may obtain mercy. For God has committed them all to disobedience, that He might have mercy on all."

In v. 30, Paul first reminds the Gentiles, that they, who were once far from the God of Abraham, Isaac, and Jacob, who were at one time pagan idolaters, have now obtained mercy from God through the preaching and receiving of the gospel of Jesus the Messiah of Israel and Savior of the world. The reason the gospel was preached to them was because Israel was disobedient to God by not accepting Jesus as their Messiah. Because of their disobedience and stubborn unbelief, a hardening or blindness came upon Israel and the Good News of Jesus went out to the Gentile world. We must not lose sight of the fact that Israel's disobedience was as a nation, and the blindness was in part. There has always been a believing remnant in Israel.

In v. 31, Paul parallels his previous statement by once again speaking of the importance of Gentiles coming to faith in Jesus and in turn leading Jewish people to faith by provoking them to jealousy. As Israel nationally rejected Jesus as their King Messiah, the gospel went to the Gentiles. As Gentiles live exemplary and praiseworthy lives as believers, showing love and mercy to Jewish people as God showed love and mercy to them, Jewish people in turn will begin to turn to Jesus until ultimately God will bring His plan for them to completion at Jesus' second coming. Stott writes:

> "It is because of disobedient Israel that disobedient Gentiles have received mercy, and it is because of this mercy to disobedient Gentiles that disobedient Jews will receive mercy too. We detect yet again the 'chain of blessing', as Israel's disobedience has led to mercy for the Gentiles which in turn will lead to mercy for Israel."[82]

In Romans 11:32 Paul concludes by summing up God's purpose and plan for both Jew and Gentile alike.

> "For God has committed them all to disobedience,
> that He might have mercy on all."

The Amplified Bible translates it this way:

> "For God has consigned (penned up) all men to disobedience, only that He may have mercy on them all [alike]."

The Greek word *sungkleioo,* translated "committed," "shut up," "bound," or "penned" has the sense of shutting in on all sides, as in a jail. Stott likens it to a "dungeon in which God has incarcerated all human beings, so that they have no possibility of escape except as God's mercy releases them."[83] This is the equivalent of Romans 3:23, "for all have sinned and fall short of the glory of God." The plight of mankind would be hopeless were it not for the mercy of God. Mills writes:

> "The Apostle places both Jew and Gentile on the same sinful ground in the presence of a holy God. Both are sinners, and are equally deserving of God's wrath and punishment. Both being guilty in God's sight, God is able to bestow His super-abounding mercy upon them both and thereby provide a way of deliverance from the quicksands of eternal death. Sin and its consequences gave occasion for the coming of the Messiah and His accomplishments on the cross. Thus our Heavenly Father provided the only possible way in which both disobedient Jew and Gentile could be delivered from the consequences of sin. This provision is the gospel."[84]

All who come to faith in Jesus the Messiah will receive the incredible, inconceivable, indescribable mercy of God.

CHAPTER 12

Theology Becomes Doxology

Paul could stop here and we would have a wonderful conclusion to the question of God's plan for Israel But Paul's heart won't allow him to stop. Just as he ended chapter eight by taking a deep breath and writing an incredibly profound and important truth of our salvation, that "nothing could separate us from the love of Christ," he now, I believe, stops and takes another deep breath and shares with us his outpouring of praise, in the form of a doxology regarding God's perfect plan of salvation for both Jew and Gentile alike. Wiersbe says, "theology becomes doxology."[85] Paul writes in Romans 11:33-36:

> "Oh, the depth of the riches both of the wisdom and knowledge of God! How unsearchable are His judgments and His ways past finding out! "For who has known the mind of the LORD? Or who has become His counselor?" 'Or who has first given to Him and it shall be repaid to him?" For of Him and through Him and to Him are all things, to whom be glory forever. Amen."

Paul is overwhelmed with joy and awe, as the particle "Oh" tells us, over God's incredible wisdom and knowledge, which to him seems so far beyond his and certainly our ability to comprehend. The plan and purpose of God for the salvation of both Jew and Gentile reveals God's infinite knowledge and His ability to use it with remarkable wisdom. He describes God's wisdom and knowledge by saying, "His judgments are unsearchable and His ways past finding out." The Greek words for "unsearchable" and "past finding out," *anexeraúneeta* and *anexichníastoi* are virtually the same. The first means "unsearchable" and the second means "untraceable." God's judgment and ways in this context refer to His decisions regarding salvation history for mankind, not His regular judicial decisions. They are unfathomable, unsearchable, untraceable, inscrutable; they are simply beyond any human beings' ability to figure out and understand.

Paul then quotes Isaiah 40:13, which reveals that God is the sole Creator of His incredible plan. No one knows His mind or gives Him advice. This quote is followed by a slightly changed quotation from Job 41:11, which testifies to God's sole responsibility for His actions. God is indeed the Sovereign of all things, the One to whom all creatures are accountable, and to whom all should give glory. Mills writes:

> "We must never forget that our God is a sovereign God, who acts, thinks, plans, and carries out His own program independent of fallible humanity. Where was man when God planned His program of salvation? Where was man when God carefully laid out His plan as recorded in Ephesians 1:4? Where was man "before the world was (John 17:5), when the holy Word went forth that the Son of God would die on the cross for sin?"[86]

Paul concludes with one final word of praise in 11:36,

> "For of Him and through Him and to Him are all things, to whom be glory forever. Amen."

Paul makes a theological affirmation of the centrality of God in all creation. He ascribes all things to God; the creation and all the creatures of creation, the redemption of mankind and all the benefits of that redemption. Stott writes:

> "These three prepositions indicate that God is the creator, sustainer, and heir of everything, its source, means and goal. He is the Alpha and Omega, and every letter of the alphabet in between."[87]

It is because all things are of, through, and to Him that glory belongs to Him and Him alone. Paul's final words in Romans 9-11 are words of love, reverence, awe, and most of all worship. His "Amen," in essence, says to us, "Let us affirm this."

The heart of the apostle went through a series of emotions in Romans 9-11. We first saw his heart broken in 9:1-2, as he had "great sorrow and continual grief in my heart," over the lostness of the people of Israel. In Romans 10:1, we saw his heart hopeful, as his "heart's desire and prayer to God for Israel is that they may be saved." In Romans 11:26 we saw Paul's heart brimming with confidence in an omnipotent, sovereign God, as he said, "All Israel will be saved." Lastly, in Romans 11:33-36 we saw the heart of the apostle rejoicing in worship as he concludes, "For of Him and through Him and to Him are all things, to whom be glory forever. Amen." To God be the glory, indeed!

End Notes

---

[1] Mills, Sanford, "A Hebrew Christian Looks at Romans," Grand Rapids, MI, Dunham Publishing Company, 1968, p. 289
[2] Moo, Douglas, "The Epistle to the Romans," Grand Rapids, MI, Wm. Eerdmans Publishing Co., 1996, p. 556
[3] Mills, P. 292
[4] Kreloff, Steven A, God's Plan For Israel: A Study of Romans 9-11, Neptune, NJ, Loizeaux Brothers, 1995, P. 21
[5] Mills, P. 293
[6] Kreloff, P. 23
[7] Mills, P. 295
[8] Moo, P. 574
[9] Mills, P.297
[10] Moo, P. 581
[11] Mills, P. 304
[12] Kreloff, P. 32
[13] Mills, P. 306
[14] Ellison, H.L., "The Mystery of Israel," London, England, The Paternoster Press, 1976, P. 50
[15] Mills, P. 313
[16] Packer, J.I., Evangelism and the Sovereignty of God, Downers Grove, Il, Inter Varsity Press, 1961, P. 35
[17] Moo, P. 601
[18] Kreloff, P. 41
[19] Stott, John, Romans, Downers Grove, IL, InterVarsity Press, 1994, P. 272
[20] Cranfield, C.E.B., The Epistle To The Romans, Vol. II, Edinburgh, T. & T. Clark Limited, 1979, pp. 496-497
[21] Mills, P. 324
[22] Moo, P. 616
[23] Moo, P. 626
[24] Mills, PP. 331-332
[25] Stott, P. 277
[26] Mills, P. 335
[27] Kreloff, P. 58
[28] Cranfield, P. 519
[29] Moo, P. 640
[30] Fruchtenbaum, Arnold, "Israelology: The Missing Link in Systematic Theology," Tustin, CA, Ariel Ministries, 1989, P. 644
[31] Fruchtenbaum, P. 644
[32] Fruchtenbaum, P.916

[33] Moo, PP. 648-649
[34] Witmer, John A., The Bible Knowledge Commentary: New Testament Edition, Romans, USA, Victor Books, 1986, P. 655
[35] Kreloff, PP. 61-62
[36] Mills, P. 341
[37] Moo, P. 660
[38] Moo, P. 663
[39] Mills, P. 347
[40] Mills, P. 349
[41] From Computer Program Warren Wiersbe's Be Series, NT, Wiersbe, Warren W, Be Right: Romans, Wheaton, IL, Victor Books
[42] Cranfield, P.
[43] Moo, P. 667
[44] Stott, P. 288
[45] Mills, P. 352
[46] Stott, P. 289
[47] Mills, P. 353
[48] Mills, P. 354
[49] Moo, P. 674
[50] Cranfield, P. 545
[51] Moo, P. 677
[52] Cranfield, PP. 547-548
[53] Mills, P. 362
[54] Stott, P. 293
[55] PC Study Bible Computer Program, Vincent's New Testament Word Studies
[56] Mills, P. 364
[57] MacArthur, John, Jr., New Testament Commentary: Romans 9-16, Chicago, IL, Moody Press, 1994, P. 104
[58] Mills, P. 365
[59] Mills, P. 367
[60] Chosen People Ministries, How To Introduce Your Jewish Friends to the Messiah, New York, New York, Chosen People Ministries, 1991, P. 13
[61] Moo, P. 689
[62] Mills, PP 368-369
[63] Moo, P. 692
[64] Witmer, P. 483-484
[65] Stott, P. 298
[66] Moo, P. 696
[67] Moo, PP. 697-698

[68] Mills, P. 372

[69] Mills, PP. 373-374
[70] Mills,, P. 374
[71] Moo, P. 704
[72] Moo, P. 705
[73] Wiersbe computer program, "Be Right," – Romans 11:16b-24

[74] Mills, P. 382
[75] Witmer, P. 485
[76] Moo, P. 710
[77] Mills, P. 385
[78] Stott, P. 304
[79] Dunn, James D. G., Word Biblical Commentary, Romans 9-16, Dallas, Texas, Word Books, 1988, P.683

[80] Mills, P. 389
[81] Stott, P. 306
[82] Stott, P. 307
[83] Ibid
[84] Mills, P. 394-395
[85] Wiersbe, Computer Program, "Be Right," Romans 11:33-36
[86] Mills, P. 397
[87] Stott, P. 311
\

Bibliography

Anderson, Leith. A Church For The 21st Century, Minneapolis, Minnesota: Bethany House Publishers, 1992.

Barnhouse, Donald Grey. Romans: Volumes 1-4, Grand Rapids, Michigan, Wm. B. Eerdmans Publishing Co, 1982.

Blaising, Craig A. The Future Of Israel As A Theological Question, Journal of the Evangelical Theological Society, Volume 44. The Evangelical Theological Society. 2001

Chapell, Bryan. Christ Centered Preaching, Grand Rapids, Michigan: Baker Books, 1994.

Cranfield, C.E.B. On Romans and Other New Testament Essays, Edinburgh, Scotland, T & T Clark, 1998.

Cranfield, C.E.B. The International Critical Commentary: Romans Vol. I &II, Edinburgh, Scotland, T & T Clark, 1979.

Dunn, James D. G. Word Biblical Commentary: Romans 9-16, Dallas, Texas, Word Publishing Co., 1988.

Decker, Bert. You've Got To Be Believed To Be Heard, New York, New York, St. Martin's Press, 1992.

Duduit, Michael, Editor. Handbook of Contemporary Preaching, Nashville, Tennessee, Broadman Press, 1992.

Ellison, H.L. The Mystery of Israel, London, England, The Paternoster Press, 1976.

Ferrin, Howard W. All Israel Shall Be Saved, Bibliotecha Sacra, Volume 112, Number 447, July, 1955.

Fruchtenbaum, Arnold G. Israelology: The Missing Link in Systematic Theology, Tustin, California, Ariel Ministries, 1989.

Galli, Mark & Larson, Craig Brian. Preaching That Connects, Grand Rapids, Michigan, Zondervan Publishing Co. 1994.

Glenny, W. Edward. The "People of God" in Romans 9:25-26, Bibliotecha Sacra, Volume 152, Number 605, January-March, 1995.

Griffith-Thomas, W.H. Commentary On Romans, Grand Rapids, Michigan, Kregel Publications, 1974.

Kreloff, Steven A. God's Plan For Israel: A Study Of Romans 9-11, Neptune, New Jersey, Loizeaux, 1995.

Lawson, Steven J. The Priority of Biblical Preaching: An Expository Study of Acts 2:42-47, Bibliotecha Sacra, Volume 158, Number 630, April-June, 2001.

Lawson, Steven J. The Power of Biblical Preaching: An Expository Study of Jonah 3:1-10, Bibliotecha Sacra, Volume 158, Number 631, July-September, 2001.

Lawson, Steven J. The Pattern of Biblical Preaching: An Expository Study of Ezra 7:10 and Nehemiah 8:1-8, Bibliotecha Sacra, Volume 158, Number 632, October-December, 2001.

Lawson, Steven J. The Passion of Biblical Preaching: An Expository Study of 1 Timothy 4:13-16, Bibliotecha Sacra, Volume 159, Number 633, January-March, 2002.

MacArthur, John Jr. The MacArthur New Testament Commentary: Romans 9-16, Chicago, Illinois, 1994.

Mawhinney, Bruce. Preaching With Freshness, Eugene, Oregon, Harvest House Publishers, 1991.

McDill, Wayne. The 12 Essential Skills For Great Preaching, Nashville, Tennessee, Broadman and Holman Publishers, 1994.

Mills, Sanford C. A Hebrew Christian Looks At Romans, Grand Rapids, Michigan, Dunham Publishing Company, 1968.

Moo, Douglas J. The Epistle To The Romans, Grand Rapids, Michigan/Cambridge, U.K.

William B. Eerdmans Publishing Company, 1996.

Murray, John. The Epistle To The Romans, Grand Rapids, Michigan/Cambridge, U.K. William B. Eerdmans Publishing Company, 1965.

Nanos, Mark D. The Mystery of Romans: The Jewish Context of Paul's Letter, Minneapolis, Minnesota, Fortress Press, 1996.

Olford, Stephen F. Anointed Expository Preaching, Nashville, Tennessee, Broadman and Holman Publishers, 1998.

Robinson, Haddon W. Biblical Preaching: The Development and Delivery of Expository Messages, Grand Rapids, Michigan, Baker Academics, 2001.

Robinson, Haddon W. Biblical Sermons: How Twelve Preachers Apply the Principles of Biblical Preaching, Grand Rapids, Michigan, Baker Book House, 1989

Robinson, Haddon W., Gibson, Scott M. Editor, Making A Difference in Preaching, Grand Rapids, Michigan, Baker Books, 1999.

Ryrie, Charles C. The End of the Law, Bibliotecha Sacra, Volume 124, Number 495, July, 1967.

Schreiner, Thomas R. Romans: Baker Exegetical Commentary on the New Testament, Grand Rapids, Michigan, Baker Books, 1998.

Shulam, Joseph. A Commentary on the Jewish Roots of Romans, Baltimore, Maryland, Messianic Jewish Publishers, 1997.

Stott, John. Romans: God's Good News For The World, Downers Grove, Illinois, InterVarsity Press, 1994.

Thiessen, Henry C. The Place of Israel in the Scheme of Redemption: As Set Forth in Romans 9-11, Part 1 Bibliotecha Sacra, Volume 98, Number 389, January, 1941.

Thiessen, Henry C. The Place of Israel in the Scheme of Redemption: As Set Forth in Romans 9-11, Part 2 Bibliotecha Sacra, Volume 98, Number 390, April, 1941.

Vines, Jerry and Shaddix Jim. Power in the Pulpit: How to Prepare and Deliver Expository Sermons, Chicago, Illinois, Moody Press, 1999.

Webb, Joseph M. Preaching Without Notes, Nashville, Tennessee, Abington Press, 2001.

Wiersbe, Warren W. Computer Program – "Be" Series NT: Be Right – The Book of Romans, Wheaton, IL, Victor Books.

Willhite, Keith and Gibson, Scott M. Editors. The Big Idea Of Biblical Preaching: Connecting the Bible to People, Grand Rapids, Michigan, Baker Books, 1998.

Williams, Philip R. Paul's Purpose in Writing Romans, Bibliotecha Sacra, Volume 128, Number 509, January, 1971.